The Complete Illustrated
WEST HIGHLAND
WHITE TERRIER

The Complete Illustrated
WEST HIGHLAND
WHITE TERRIER

Edited by

Joe and Liz Cartledge

With contributions by

G. B. DENNIS
BARBARA GRAHAM
JOHN HOLMES
CATHERINE OWEN
BETTY PENN-BULL
MICHAEL STOCKMAN

Ebury Press · London

First published 1973
by Ebury Press
Chestergate House, Vauxhall Bridge Road
London SW1V 1HF

ISBN 0 85223 043 5

All photographs by Angela Cavill unless otherwise indicated

Photoset in Great Britain by
Typesetting Services Ltd, Glasgow
and printed and bound by
Interlitho s.p.a., Milan, Italy

Contents

The Editors

JOE CARTLEDGE

It would be right to say that Joe Cartledge has been concerned with
pedigree dogs and dog shows all his life. Before the First World
War and between the two wars his uncle, the late Arthur Cartledge,
was one of the foremost dog handlers in Britain and in the United
States. It was in these surroundings and environment that Joe
developed his love for the dog game. Except for his years in the
services in the Second World War dogs have been his whole life,
first as a boy with his uncle, and then as kennelman with the world
famous Crackley Terrier Kennels. In 1949 he started his own
kennels and handled dogs for many of the top people in the dog
world throughout the fifties, winning championships in eleven
different breeds, including Dog of the Year award on two
occasions, and Best in Show with an Airedale Terrier at Cruft's,
the world's most important dog show, in 1961. He retired from
handling at the end of 1961 as he found that the handling of dogs
both here and on the Continent, his writing and judging both in
Britain and abroad he was becoming too diversified. He now judges
almost every week in Britain, and has judged in Hong Kong,
Ceylon, Singapore, Malaysia, Australia, New Zealand, Rhodesia,
Zambia, The Republic of South Africa, Brazil, Argentina, Uruguay
Finland, Sweden, Norway, Denmark, Italy, Germany, Switzerland
and Holland. He contributes a weekly column in *Dog World,* the
top weekly paper devoted to pedigree dogs. He is Chairman of
Ryslip Kennels Ltd., and of Ryslip Livestock Shipping Company.
He edits and publishes the *Dog Directory* and *Dog Diary.*

LIZ CARTLEDGE

Although young in years, Liz, like her husband, has also spent her
entire life with dogs. She was born in Gothenburg, Sweden, to
parents who were both concerned with the exhibiting and training
of dogs, mainly Dobermanns and Boxers. She came to England
first in 1964 as a kennel student with the Dreymin Kennels of
Beagles, Bassets and Corgis. Later, and until her marriage, she was
on the editorial staff of *Dog World.* A dog judge herself, she travels
the world as secretary to her husband, one of the busiest judges in
the world today.

1 The Westie as a Pet

BY BARBARA GRAHAM

So you want a West Highland White Terrier. You have
been checking up on the breeds which are available. You
consider that this game little fellow with the roguish
expression, dark eyes and white coat looks very appealing.
You could just be right, as many town and country households have over the last ten or more years found out. The
West Highland White Terrier is now one of the most
popular of all terrier breeds. With the ever increasing cost
of feeding the pet, the comparatively smaller homes we
now live in, the smaller garden space and the built up areas
have all helped to make this little short-legged terrier a
great favourite. Though not a lap dog by any stretch of the
imagination, he readily adapts himself to the family and
can easily be picked up and tucked under the arm. The
general standard of the breed tells us that he is possessed
with no mean amount of self esteem. He is strongly built
and deep in chest with a level back and powerful quarters.
It is those beady eyes which peer mischievously from under
their white lashes that give him his hard varminty
expression. He is a true terrier, and that's for sure, full of
character, intensely curious and with an obstinate streak
that seems to stem from the curiosity which must be
satisfied before he finds what you want from him. He will
walk you off your feet and when you have collapsed
exhausted into your armchair he will ask to be let out to
chase the next door neighbour's cat who he suspects is
trespassing in his garden. At other times, and just to give
you an insight to the other side of his nature, he will be
content to sit on your lap, or sleep peacefully at your feet
and dream of those ginger toms making faces at him from
behind the potting shed. Let us consider his other
attributes, though I hasten to add that I am not trying to
sell you a Westie. What I am trying to do is to help you
find out if this sporting little fellow is the pet most suitable
for you and your family. Size-wise the Westie is most
suitable for any modern home. In the country, or in a
home in town with a sizable garden this game little terrier
will be in his element. Although he is capable of walking

any normal human into the ground, with a reasonably sized and securely fenced garden he will be quite happy to exercise himself, with only an occasional walk on the lead. In town, of course, and if you are a flat dweller, the situation is somewhat different. In this case, unless at least one person in the family is happy to see that he gets his exercise on the lead and additional time off the lead in the local park, chasing a ball maybe, I would like to suggest a dog from the toy group – the Yorkie, Pekingese or Maltese.

Another chapter in this book has been set aside to deal with the trimming, grooming and general presentation of the coat, so it is sufficient for me just to touch on the matter. Though the Westie's coat is comparatively long, he does not shed his coat or moult twice a year all over your carpet and furniture like short smooth-coated dogs. Like the Wire Fox Terrier, the Welsh Terrier, the Airedale and a number of other breeds, the Westie has what is termed a 'broken coat', a double coat consisting of a soft undercoat and a hard outer coat. Because of this weather resistant coat, even in the coldest time of the year it is not necessary to make this hardy fellow look foolish by fitting him out with one of those tartan or multi-coloured jackets one sometimes sees. Finally, I would like to mention, and sincerely hope that it will be remembered, that the Westie coat has a certain amount of waterproofing oil in its make-up, and therefore too much bathing is not advisable. Brushing and combing are a must, and if adopted as a regular habit they not only invigorate the hair and encourage both healthy hair and skin, they help in no small way to keep the animal free from skin infection. Apart from this they will make the job of trimming, when the time comes around, much easier, and the finished job look much better and more professional.

It could be that I am just a bit biased because for the last twenty-six years there has always been at least one Westie in my home, but to me the Westie is the ideal family pet. He is small, game, very alive and most intelligent, easy to feed, condition and groom. A man's dog that is loved and admired by the ladies and certainly a great favourite with

the children. Let us assume that you have not put the cart
before the horse. You have bought this book on the West
Highland White Terrier before you have actually made a
purchase. You are one of the wise ones. Although *you* are
completely sold on the idea of owning one, you are not as
yet convinced that the whole family are with you in this
choice. Take the family with you to make the choice.
Hundreds of Westie puppies and adults are sold each year
but it is not always possible to locate a good Westie
breeding kennels when the time comes, and it is my wish
to put you in touch with well-proved genuine breeders.
It is true that there are many good reliable pet shops and
dealers, but when buying livestock of any kind cut out
the middleman if at all possible. The breeder, and breeder
only, is in a position to let you see the puppy's dam and
possibly both the parents. They are able to tell you the
puppy's correct age; able to tell you what the puppy has
been fed on and in what amounts since it was weaned;
they can give you a diet sheet and a pedigree which are
worth the paper they are written on. If you go to the
horse's mouth, you will be able to see that the puppy
has had its necessary wormings and inoculations. Lastly,
if anything goes wrong with your puppy, you have only
to go back to the breeder. If you go to the middleman he
will refer you to the breeder, who is possibly going to tell

you that it's not his responsibility. The pup was okay
when it left his kennels. You will more than likely finish
up running around in ever-decreasing circles, spending
money for veterinary services that would not have been
spent if you had gone to a breeder. Any breeder who is
worth his salt will always be willing to help with a puppy
he or she has sold – an after-sales service is always yours
if you go to a breeder of repute.

'But how do we get an introduction and in touch with
such a breeder? I'm sure we don't have one in our locality.'
That's a good question. You are quite right, this is sometimes a problem. You see, breeders of Westies, or any other
breed for that matter, are not making a fortune from
breeding. Their kennels are invariably run on a shoestring
budget, in fact at the end of the breeding season they are,
in most cases, lucky if they have broken even. Not for them
expensive advertising when they have a litter of puppies
for sale. Neither do they have a shop window like the pet
shop or the large store. The proud and worthwhile breeder
wouldn't be interested in displaying his live wares in such
a way in any case. From your newsagent you can order,
even if you are not able to purchase over the counter,
Dog World or *Our Dogs*, both weekly publications for the
pedigree dog which carry 'Puppies for sale' advertising.
From most good booksellers you are also able to get the
Dog Directory. I suggest you write directly to the editor who
also publishes the book at Binfield Park, Bracknell,
Berkshire. At the establishments you are able to find in
these publications you will be able to make your choice
from the whole litter. Beware of putting your deposit on
the little runt who backs away into the corner when you
visit the kennel or the run to see him. The mortality rate
of these little waifs is very high. Buy the one with the
bright eye, fit-looking coat, and with no pot belly which
looks as if it is full of worms. Do not be tempted to take the
pup away from its home until it is at least eight weeks old.
In any case a reputable breeder would not allow you to do
so, as the puppy is usually weaned completely at the age of
seven weeks and taken away from his mother. By the end
of the eighth week the breeder has satisfied himself that

the pup is capable of standing on his own feet and can feed well without resorting to Mum. You may find he is difficult to feed at first because he has not got the competition, of his brothers and sisters – or the little rascal is far too interested in his new surroundings – but stick to the diet sheet for the first few months. Naturally breeders vary slightly in their mode of feeding but the basic idea is the same in that a nutritious diet at regular hours gives the new puppy a good start and builds a healthy dog for the future. An eight-week-old puppy needs five meals a day. First thing in the morning I suggest a quarter of a pint of warm milk mixed with a baby cereal to a thin gruel con- sistency, and sweetened with a little honey or glucose. As a variation he can have milky porridge or any breakfast cereal. At mid-day he needs a meat meal of two ounces of minced meat, heart, rabbit or ox cheek. Soak about a tablespoon of puppy meal in bone stock or vegetable stock and mix together. After lunch about 2 o'clock give him a saucer of warm milk. The six o'clock meal is the same as mid-day. Last thing at night again a quarter of a pint of warm milk mixed with the baby food and half a raw egg. He also needs extra calcium to aid development of bones and teeth at this early age. Dogs do not absorb calcium in its natural state unless it is balanced with phosphorus so it is advisable to include in his diet the product the breeder has been using. The quantities should be increased so that the dog should have six to eight ounces of meat daily. The first meal your pup will refuse will be the plain milk and by about four months he should be having three meals a day, at six months two meals and when he is a year old he will be content with one. Always feed a pup or adult with biscuit meal that has been scalded with boiling stock as the meal swells and should not be allowed to swell inside the dog. If allowed to do so it is liable to cause digestive troubles. Although I do not altogether hold with tinned food I do feel it is advisable for your pup to be 'introduced' to the more meaty varieties on the market. Then when and if an emer- gency arises there is always something for him. Unchopped marrow bones, even though they are nearly as big as he is, will give untold joy and are helpful with cutting teeth.

Keep your pup on the plump side, as he only grows once, and if you underfeed him you will starve his nerves and will end up with a nervous highly-strung dog. By the time he is a year old his water bowl can remain on the floor so he can drink when he wants; at an earlier age I find my youngsters will insist on using it as a paddling pool! The adult dog should not be allowed to get fat and if you put your hand on his neck and come down his body you should be just able to feel his ribs beneath your fingers. If you are a complete novice it is quite a good idea to let your veterinary surgeon who you have chosen to inoculate and advise you throughout the dog's lifetime, go over your new buy. At the same time let it be known to the breeder that this is your intention either on the way home or the following day. It has been known for a breeder when told this to refuse to sell, an indication surely that all is not well. If this is the case I suggest you don't try to follow up with the sale anyway. On the other hand, on

being given a clean bill of health by the veterinary surgeon, ask his advice on future inoculations. Remember, the veterinary surgeon, if you have chosen wisely, is your dog's best friend. If you don't consider you have chosen wisely, change. You are quite within your rights to change your butcher or grocer, and so you are to change your vet if you are not satisfied with the service he is giving you and your pet.

As a breed the Westie is a great dog for car travelling. He will soon be taught to guard the car too, if that is what you require of him. Also he can be taught to take a back seat. In many countries children and dogs are not allowed by law to sit in the front, in my opinion a sound law indeed. When introducing the puppy into your home a number of things must be remembered. Everything to him is strange. He has just left his home, the place he thought was the entire world until that very day. Gosh! But it's a large world and very frightening and he must be allowed to

relax for a time. The family have been looking forward to
his arrival for weeks, maybe months, and the children –
particularly the children – must not at this stage be
allowed to give this possibly bewildered youngster a
welcoming party. A quiet understanding word, a dish of
milk maybe. Food at this stage should not be forced on
him. A bowl of water and a bed where you intend him to
sleep and have his rests should be ready in place. He
should be allowed to explore on his own the place which is

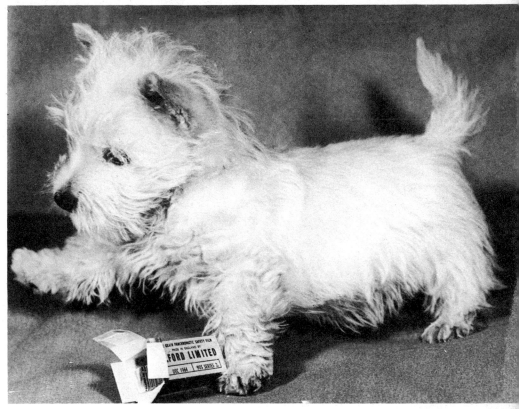

to be his future home. Dog beds can be bought at dog
shows and in some pet stores, but if you are a handyman,
or have a 'Do It Yourself' man about the place, a practical
sleep bed can be made from simple materials available
in Do It Yourself shops. It might be a good idea, however,
to use a large cardboard box in the first place. In the
first few weeks it could be quite expensive if he takes to
chewing. Use the box as it is, folding the top in so that
it forms a cube and then cut a hole in one side big enough
for him to get in and out easily. If the hole is cut above the
level of the floor it will prevent draughts and he will be snug
and warm in it. Give him a special treat to go to bed for
the night, a blanket or layers of newspaper, put him inside
the box and shut the door. Put cottonwool in your ears and
do not go down until the morning. He may howl or bark,
or both for the first night or possibly two, but if you can
stand it, and you don't give in, you'll win and will then
have no further trouble. Give in and allow him to be on

your bed – oh yes, he's so small and helpless – and that is where he will have to sleep for the rest of his natural . . . you are his slave. Do start as you mean to carry on as far as training is concerned. Training is quite easy if you do not allow him to get into bad habits first. Choose a place in the garden, out of the way, yet easy to get at, disinfect and occasionally dig over. Then after a meal, when he makes a mistake on the carpet or any other place indoors, first thing in the morning or last thing at night, take him at once to the place you have set aside for him to use as a toilet. In a few days in many cases, or with some puppies a little longer, he will be crying and scratching at the door to get out and relieve himself. With a pet in a flat, particularly in an upstairs flat or apartment, the same rules apply though the operation will have to be carried out in a slightly different way. The 'flat' puppy must right away be taught to be clean and go to do his toilet on newspaper spread out on the floor in a suitable corner. Again the handyman can come into his own by making a flat box or tray. Covered with newspaper, the tray can easily be kept clean, disinfected, and fresh.

Even from as early as eight or nine weeks old a five minute grooming will not come amiss, if only to teach the youngster to stand for the job of being groomed and trimmed when he is older.

As I have said before *I* am a bit biased with regard to the West Highland; but before you buy make very sure that you and your family are certain he is the dog for you.

BARBARA GRAHAM

Mrs Graham has been associated with West Highland White Terriers for most of her life and, in fact, started to breed and exhibit them twenty-six years ago. From these small beginnings Mrs Graham and her Lasara Westies have become famous the world over. The Lasaras made their first champion in the breed in 1963, and in 1967 were Best of Breed at Cruft's Dog Show. The Lasaras have been exported with outstanding success since the early sixties to many countries of the world including America, Canada, South Africa and a number of countries on the Continent. Many of these terriers have gained the title of champion in

Mrs Graham with one of her famous Lasara Westies

the country of their adoption, and it would not be exaggerating to say that Mrs Graham's International Champion Lasara Lennie was one of the great founders of the West Highland White Terrier breed in Sweden. Mrs Graham started judging the breed at championship level in 1965, and officiated at the West Highland Club of Ireland in 1970, the National Terrier Show at Leicester in 1971 and has been asked to officiate at Cruft's Dog Show in 1974.

2 The History and Origins of the Westie
BY G. B. DENNIS

As far back as 1870 Colonel Malcolm of Poltalloch has been quoted as saying that these little white dogs had been known for a century or more at Poltalloch and that they were a breed with a very long pedigree and not an invented breed of that time. They were kept as hard-working terriers and valued for their toughness and ability to deal with any vermin such as badgers, otters, foxes, wild cats or rabbits which were to be found in those western Highlands of Scotland. Amongst the crags and rocks and into the very small burrows beneath they were in their element. Further back than one can trace it can only be imagined that they must have come of a very mixed bunch of short-legged terriers which, according to the demands made of them in later years, developed into at least three types. There seems little doubt that the Aberdeens, or the Scots as they later became better known, and the smaller brindled Cairn and the White Poltalloch (as they were most commonly called in the early days) originated from the same source. The whites were also known as the Rosenneaths but in due course it was decided that as they were so closely associated with the Western Highlands of Scotland they should thereafter be known as the West Highland White Terrier. However, it took a long time before the name Poltalloch was finally dropped. I remember at the very first Cruft's Show I ever attended at the Agricultural Hall at Islington, an elderly Scottish gentleman approached me as I was replacing my dog on the bench and said to me, 'That's a right bonnie Poltalloch you have there'. When I replied that it was a West Highland White Terrier he glared at me fiercely and growled, 'Yon's a Poltalloch'. Later I wished I had held him in conversation and found out more of what he knew about the breed in its earlier years, for he looked the sort that had probably known them very well and worked them in their natural surroundings.

It is hard to describe how so much strength and determination could be contained in such a small frame, the ideal weight at that time being between sixteen and eighteen pounds for a male and a little less for a female.

Colonel Malcolm of Poltalloch

Height at the withers was anything between eight to twelve inches which left room for a great deal of doubt about the ideal size. This, as we will find out, was altered many years later when the standard was revised. That these small dogs could tackle a fox and hold on to it seems incredible but they were hardly reared for the purpose and well and truly fulfilled their task. This was before they became too well known as show dogs. It is said that it was thought of no consequence to take a dog to shows in the early days with half an ear missing and showing many other battle scars from days spent hunting. In fact, these scars were displayed more as an award of great merit than anything else. Tough as they were at work, they were ideal companions on long winter's nights before a glowing peat fire, obedient and quick to make friends with people to whom they had been properly introduced, but woe betide any intruder who dared venture inside uninvited. This is still true today when I look on my Westies as my guards; they will let no one past until I give the word.

In Glasgow in 1860 there were classes for 'Scotch Terriers' which seems to have included any short-legged terrier of Scotland. In 1899 a white Scottish Terrier owned by Lady A. Forbes was among the winners at the Crystal Palace show. West Highlands were first separately classified at the Scottish Kennel Club show held in Waverley Market in Edinburgh in October 1904. Morven, owned by Mr Colin Young from Fort William, was the first champion of the breed. From then on the breed started on its upward trend and, of course, as it became known for all its great qualities as a worker, and even more as a wonderful companion in the house, and as a most distinctive dog for show purposes, it began to get more and more popular. As they became better known in the show ring it is easy to see from the old pictures of the breed that as time went on they were being shielded from too much field work to enable them to be presented with a more profuse coat on their head and body, to present a more distinguished appearance show-wise. Yet no matter what is done to them to turn them into sophisticated show dogs, the natural instinct of the hunter is always there, as anyone will soon discover if they can still find a few acres of unspoilt countryside where there may still be found the scent of fox or rabbit. Westies' dominant hunting streak will quickly come uppermost and regardless of future show dates they will go through the thickest hedge regardless, stripping every hair from their heads or legs. To them sport is still the supreme reason for living. As Colonel Malcolm of Poltalloch said, 'The West Highland of the old sort – I do not of course speak of bench dogs – earn their living following fox, badger and otter wherever they went, underground, between, over or under rocks that no man could get at to move, and some of such a size that a hundred men could not move them. I want my readers to understand this and not to think of a Highland fox cairn as

Westie with a Scottie friend

if it was an English fox earth dug in sand: nor of badger as if it was a question of locating the badger and digging him out. No, the badger makes his home among rocks, the smaller ones weighing perhaps two or three tons and probably he has his hinner end against one of three or four hundred tons – no digging him out – and moreover the passages between the rocks must be taken as they are; no scratching them a little wider. So if the dog's ribs are a trifle too big he may squeeze one or two through the narrow slit and then stick. He will never be able to pull himself back until reduced by starvation so that he can regain his freedom.'

Here we have the true reason why the Westie has his heart-shaped ribs, giving the appearance of a flat-sided dog. The much talked of 'spring of rib' is from the back bone from where it descends in a heart shape and not as in the Scottie with its barrel-shaped ribs. The Westie has rather broad shoulder blades, closely knit at the withers, a medium length of back with a nice span across the loin combined with the hard sinewy and well-boned legs and feet wherein lies the great strength needed for its digging activities. This sturdy body is well protected against the fury of its antagonists by the strength of its jaws which seem extraordinarily powerful for such a small dog, with damaging teeth that can kill a huge rat with one bite. Its second protection is its wonderful double coat, the top coat being hard and weather resistant and has certain (though not visible) amount of oiliness which can throw off rain like its owner's weatherproof, the undercoat is warm and woolly. Any Westie without its double coat is at a great disadvantage with its better clad brethren at work in the wolds, and loses many points in the show ring when presented with an 'open' coat. This good double coat also enables the dog to penetrate the roughest bramble and bracken without getting unduly damaged, and the ruff, which was always left uncut in the olden days in great profusion around the neck, must have saved many a dog from having its throat torn by a foe. Nowadays it is considered smarter for show purposes to trim out the thickest part of this which, it must be admitted, does show up a lovely neck line, but at the same time it does, unless well done, expose any faults that would be better hidden.

The first three champions were made up in 1907, the first being Morven owned by Mr Colin Young and the other two Ch. Cromar Snowflake by Morven out of Snowdrift, and Ch. Oronsay, by Conas out of Jean, both owned by the Countess of Aberdeen. These, together with their contemporaries, laid the foundation of the breed. That year one hundred and forty one dogs and bitches were registered. Many famous names are brought to mind as one looks back

over very old pedigrees. Mr J. Campbell who produced
many champions owning the Oronsay prefix, Mrs Cameron
Head who worked and showed her dogs with marked
success; Mrs B. Lucas who bred many champions and
whose Highclere prefix is still to be found in some of the
older pedigrees.

The one name that stands out above all others in any
period of the breed must surely be that of Mrs May Pacey
with the longest line of champions which no one in the
breed is ever likely to surpass. The prefix of 'Wolvey' was
held in the very highest regard as was Mrs Pacey herself
as a breeder and international judge, and a wonderful
personality who was always ready with help and advice to
the newcomer. Before her marriage she had kept other
breeds and been successful with Sealyhams, but gradually
she turned to her one great love, West Highland Whites.
As fast as she made up one champion there would be
another youngster just biding its time to come in and steal
the limelight. Her first champion was Ch. Wolvey Piper,
bred in Skye. She always considered that Ch. Wolvey
Patrician was one of the greatest she had ever bred and he
was an outstanding sire. Her lovely bitch Ch. Wolvey
Pintail was another one never to be forgotten, which made
Best in Show on more than one occasion. Mrs Pacey never
lost her enthusiasm for the breed. She must have bred over
fifty champions in her time, many of which went to
America and other countries and set many people up in the
breed. Mrs E. A. Beels made her first champion Dud
O'Petriburg in 1935. After the war she bought Calluna the
Poacher from Miss A. Wright; Poacher, a wonderful dog
who lived to ripe old age, became a most famous champion
and sired a great many other champions.

A contemporary of Mrs Pacey was Mrs Winnie Barber
who jointly owned the well-known prefix 'Scotia' with her
father, the great Holland Buckley; both were internationally
famous as breeders and terrier judges.

In the years between 1929 and 1939 the 'Rushmoors',
owned by Miss Smith-Wood, made an indelible mark both
here and in the United States. After becoming a champion
here Ch. Ray of Rushmoor was sold to America where he

quickly gained his championship and after siring many champions there returned to England to carry on the good work at stud. A grand dog in every way, a beautiful head, short back, sturdily built, with the stamp of quality written all over him. There were many other Rushmoor champions but none ever quite so famous as Ray. Then of course Miss Audrey Wright who was of true Scottish descent and knew just what was required of a genuine West Highland produced Ch. Calluna Ruairidh whose name figures in nearly all of the older pedigrees. To be breeder of the famous Ch. Calluna the Poacher should have been achievement enough for anyone, but of course there were many other good ones to come from the same source.

Mrs Hewson with her 'Clints' did a lot for the breed with her champions Chief, Topper, Cyrus, Cocktail, Cheek and others. Mrs Allom with her very good dogs made a deep impression and did much good to the breed with her 'Furzefields' and particularly with Furzefield Piper who, although not a champion because of a misplaced tooth, sired at least seven champions. Among the most famous of these was Ch. Hookwood Mentor owned by Miss Ella Wade, daughter of the great professional handler Arthur Wade. Mentor's most famous son was undoubtedly Ch. Barrister of Branston who sired a great many champions and whose name is in the pedigrees of Glengyles, Kendrums, Quakertowns, O'Petriburgs, Famechecks and many others. There are so many names of people who had good dogs that it is impossible to mention them all. It should not be forgotten that Ch. Melbourne Mathias, bred by Miss M. Turnbull (Leal) was in the background of many of the afore-mentioned dogs. This is clearly seen in the family trees within the book of 'The West Highland White Terrier' written by D. Mary Dennis.

Dr and Mrs Russell of 'Cruben' fame bred many more good ones of which the best was undoubtedly English and American champion Cruben Dextor. In this time in America he sired a very great number of champion Westies. After the end of the Second World War Miss T. Rollo bought Timoshenko of the Roe from Mrs Garnett in Ireland and that I think was the beginning of the 'Kendrum' kennel as far as show dogs were concerned (although Miss Rollo, being Scottish, would almost certainly have kept them before this time). Timoshenko was Best in Show at the first club show held at Peterborough after the war and what an entry there was for Mrs Winnie Barber to judge! The 'Kendrums' were to be responsible for many good champions after that, the best known of which was Ch. Eoghan of Kendrum, son of Ch. Barrister of Branston. Mrs Pat Welch bought Freshney Fray from Mrs McKinney and that was her first champion after the 'Glengyle' dogs. At one time in her small but selective kennel no fewer than six out of eight Westies were champions – something to be proud of. In the North Mrs Sansom's 'Quakertowns' have brought out several champions; the most famous was undoubtedly Ch. 'Q' Quistador. Miss S. Cleland's 'Birkfells' in Westmorland were well known as outstanding bitch champions.

Mrs Granville Ellis, who had spent her life amongst Westies, had many champions, and I remember well her lovely Ch. Slitrig Shining star of Lynwood. Mrs Finch's 'Shiningcliff' made a good start by breeding Shiningcliff Simon in her first litter; he became a champion in 1947 and also went Best in Show at the S.K.C. show in Glasgow. Mrs Finch subsequently made seven more champions before she retired in 1959.

Miss F. Cook made her first champion in 1954. Ch. Famecheck Lucky Charm, certainly well named, was sired by Ch. Shiningcliff Sultan out of her first home-bred bitch, Famecheck Paddy Scalare. After that there seems to have been an inexhaustible supply of champions bred in this kennel.

Several good champions came from Mrs C. Kirby's 'Slitrigs'. Although she only kept a small number she made her first champion in 1955. It is interesting to note how many champions came from kennels of restricted size, proving that quality not quantity counts most. A good foundation bitch bred to the most suitable dog after serious study of both pedigrees is the answer. Indiscriminate breeding is a waste of time because only once in a blue moon will anything worth while result.

There are so many other names that should be mentioned like Mr and Mrs B. Thompson with their Waideshouse champions Woodpecker, Warrant, Woodlark, Waterboy and many others. Mrs B. Graham, in partnership with her mother Mrs Hazell, jointly owned the 'Lasara' prefix and made their first champion in 1963. Mrs M. Lemon's 'Citrus' has made two champions.

In the last ten years many younger ones have come along to take the place of the old stagers. Mrs Bertram with the 'Highstiles', Mrs Sylvia Kearsey with the 'Pillertons', Miss C. Owen's 'Gaywyn', the Rev. Michael Collings 'Purston', whose exports to America are enjoying much success. Mrs M. Coy started with a dog sent out to her in Canada by Mrs. Beer of 'Whitebriar' fame, who subsequently became Canadian Ch. Whitebriar Jamie. Later Mrs Coy returned to England where her prefix 'Cedarfell' soon became prominent in the show ring. In 1972 her Ch. Merry 'N'

Bright was the top winning Westie of the year. Mrs S. Morgan's 'Ballacoar', with two champions, looks to have a promising future. Mrs Audrey Millen who owns the 'Sarmac' prefix has also done very well with Ch. Lindenhall Drambuie and Ch. Heathstream Drummer Boy. Finally Mrs R. B. Pritchard has made a start with Ch. Melwyn Pillerton Picture. The West Highland White Terrier Club and The West Highland White Terrier Club (of England) were both formed in 1905. The breed standard was drawn up in about 1908 and revised in 1948 when the height was altered to eleven inches at the shoulder and the weight standard eliminated. The number of registrations at the Kennel Club is now approaching five thousand.

G. B. DENNIS

I don't expect to be contradicted by anyone connected with the breeding and exhibiting of West Highland White Terriers when I state that there is no one living today who is more qualified to write on the history of the Westie than Mr G. B. Dennis. Long before he was born, his father, Mr Nelson F. Dennis, was a breeder and exhibitor of this Scottish breed. Our writer himself exhibited his first Westie in the early twenties, and shortly after his father's death, along with his mother he registered the kennel prefix 'Owton.' The Owton prefix was allowed to lapse, and on his marriage the now world-renowned prefix of 'Branston' was born. It was not very long before the Dennis's and the name of Branston became a word one thought of first in the breed.

Mr Dennis undertook his first judging engagement in 1946 and since this first appointment his services as a judge of the breed have been continually sought after. Elected to the committee of the West Highland White Terrier Club in the same year, Mr Dennis has held office ever since, and was elected by popular vote to the position of president in 1971. He was a founder member of the London and Home Counties Terrier Club and was elected chairman from which post he retired in 1972.

J.C.

3 Trimming of the Westie
BY CATHERINE OWEN

As this chapter is being written for those who are confused as to when, where, how and why to strip a Westie, I hope the explanations will be easily understood by the novice and the photographs will give an idea of what you are trying to achieve.

Firstly, I would like to quote the Westie breed standard on coat. 'Colour pure white, must be double coated. The outer coat consists of hard hair about two inches long, free from any curl. The undercoat, which resembles fur, is short and close. Open coats are objectionable.'

Those who truly appreciate good texture in coat would never resort to cutting it. If the hair is cut in any way the roots are left in the skin, thereby choking the growth of new hair and causing irritation of the skin. Consequently, the coat which comes through is fine, soft, has no texture and will also cause a skin irritation. If the stripping is done by pulling the hairs with the finger and thumb, you are getting it out by the roots. Where each root comes out, there is room for new hairs to grow through. This encourages a good, hard, thick coat to grow. Even a poorly coated puppy can be improved if worked on regularly. The art in trimming is to make a dog look natural. In the early days, possibly the only trimming consisted of hair being pulled out by the dogs as they hunted through the undergrowth. Today there is a tendency for necks to be over-trimmed, shoulders shaved down, furnishings cut straight, ears clipped and heads to look as if a pudding basin has been put over and cut round. Westies are not a carved out breed so do not chop and hack at their coat. Scissors are useful tools but do not become addicted to them. Use them only sparingly and never leave any scissored lines. Once you get used to hand trimming, it will not take any longer. Try it and see! A properly trimmed Westie is a work of art and once this has been achieved, a great deal of personal satisfaction rewards the effort.

Trimming should preferably be done by daylight rather than artificial light and on a good solid table of suitable

A very untidy Westie in need of a trim

height, so that you can work on your dog easily and not strain your back. Have a piece of rubber matting attached to the table to keep the dog from slipping and sliding around while you work (a rubber car mat will do).

The Necessary Tools
Blunt stripping knife with coarse teeth.
Fine toothed pen knife.
Hair-dressing scissors – Ama 999 blue steel 7″.
Serrated scissors – Ama blue steel 23 teeth.
Rounded and curved scissors.
Steel combs – Spratts No. 70 and No. 71.
Rake brush.
Dolling-up pad.
Nail clippers.
Nail file.
Chalk or Bob Martin's Cleansfur.
Rubber office finger or finger stalls to get a grip on the hair.
PATIENCE – the most important thing of all.

Whether keeping a puppy for potential show purposes or as
a pet, it is essential that it learns to be groomed regularly.
Start grooming the puppy at six or eight weeks old. There
is, of course, little coat to groom at this stage but it
accustoms the puppy to being handled. If the coat is
allowed to get tangled, combing will hurt the puppy, who
naturally resents it. Particular attention should be paid to
the hair under the armpits, thighs, down the legs and
around the feet where mats are liable to form. It is very
unkind to let a dog get matted and if groomed regularly, it
takes barely five minutes to do it thoroughly. The comb
must go right through the coat down to the skin and not
just over the top of the hair. The head furnishings should
be combed forward over the face, leg hair combed down. A
good groom does a lot for the comfort of the puppy as it
gets older, as it removes dead dry hair, scurf and dirt,
stimulates the blood circulation and helps prevent skin
trouble. As dogs are unable to tell you if they are in pain,
grooming sessions are the times that you can spot trouble
starting.

Older dogs tend to accumulate tartar around the necks of
teeth, which can turn them a dirty brown colour causing
bad breath. Occasionally, foreign bodies such as twigs,
particles of food, paper or even pieces of bone get jammed
in between the teeth and cause decay. Signs of pain in the
mouth are the dog rubbing its face along the ground,
pawing the mouth, holding the head on one side or salivat-
ing. If the teeth are very bad, loose, or if the gums are
inflamed the dog should be treated by a Veterinary Surgeon.
(Large marrow bones or hard biscuits will help remove
some tartar.)

Another problem that should be watched is the anal
glands. The dog has two anal sacs, one on each side of the
anus. They sometimes become clogged with their own
secretions and may become infected. If the dog slides its
hindquarters on the ground or it bites or chews at its rear,
it is a sign of impaction. Impacted anal sacs should be
emptied by grasping the tail with the left hand and, using
the thumb and forefinger of the right hand, gently squeeze
just below the centre of the dog's anus. The contents,

which have a vile odour, should be squeezed into a paper towel or large piece of cotton wool. An abscess may develop if this is not done.

If the dog is found to be licking its paws, this is often a sign of inflammation caused by interdigital cysts or grass seeds caught between the toes and can be very sore if not dealt with quickly. Check through the coat for external parasites such as fleas, lice, ticks, harvest mites, etc. Ears and eyes are other important places to look. All these points can so easily be spotted during regular grooming sessions and can save the dog a lot of inconvenience and unnecessary suffering.

The care of toenails is another thing that is so often neglected and can spoil an otherwise well-kept dog. Long nails are solely the result of bad kennel management. The nails need gradual and frequent trimming. As the quick reaches nearly to the end of the nail, it is easy to cut in to the quick, causing bleeding when the nail is long. If bleeding does occur, potassium permanganate crystals can

Clipping the toenails

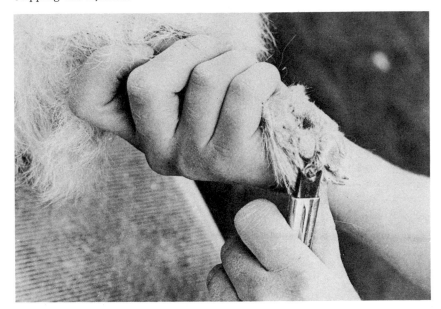

be applied to restrict it. Whereas on black nails the quick cannot be seen, it shows up pink on white nails. Cut the points off the nails including the dew claws if they have not been removed and then use a steel file to take off the rough edges. If the quicks are cut, it will subsequently become a battle royal every time the dog's feet are touched. The frequency of cutting depends on the type of exercise the dog receives, whether on grass or concrete, and on the way in which the nails grow. Some may need trimming weekly and others not as frequently.

It must be remembered that dogs, like children, have temper tantrums and it is imperative that you are always in control of the dog and show him who is boss! Always

Pulling out untidy hair (see page 45)

be gentle but firm and never hurt or injure the puppy and he will really love the fuss and attention during his grooming sessions.

First Trim

At eight weeks the puppy is ready for his first trim. If you have bought the puppy from a breeder this will have been done when you collect him. If you have bred him yourself, then this is the time for you to start work. The long fluffy hair should be pulled off the top third of both the inside and outside of the ears, under the throat in the region of the Adam's apple, in a triangle down to the chest bone and around to the points of the shoulder (you will be able to feel these bones quite well). The easiest way to do this is to rub a little chalk into the hair making it easier to grip, being very careful that none goes into the ears as this will cause irritation. Then with the index finger and thumb or fine-toothed pen knife, pull out the long hairs, just a few at a time until it is nice and even. Next cut out the hair between the pads to stop the feet from spreading. Curved scissors are used so that if the puppy moves the points will not dig into the foot. Comb the hair down around the feet and trim the long hairs that extend beyond the pads on both front and back feet, being very careful not to cut too high and get holes between the legs and feet. Scissor around the anus cutting the hair close, to keep the puppy clean, and blend in the rest of the hair on the hind quarters with the side furnishings, using the stripping knife to give a nice flat bottom. Finally, neaten the tail, pulling the long hairs first and then finishing with straight scissors to point the end.

The first puppy fluff which begins to stand out and look untidy on the back should be removed at the age of about three or four months. It is always easier to trim after chalking the dog as you get a better grip on the coat, so brush the chalk well into the coat. Next grip the puppy firmly with the left hand holding slightly above the area being stripped to keep the skin taut. With the right hand, thumb and index finger, pull out a few hairs at a time with quick sharp jerks. Only the long hard coat should be pulled, not the soft under-coat, otherwise the puppy will be bald. Follow the growth of hair, never going against the grain. Finger and thumb is the best method as then there is no risk of cutting the ends of the hair, but a blunt stripping knife can be used with care. Strip from behind the ears and back of the head down the back to the tail, from the top of the front leg above the elbow to the base of the tail, under the throat and down the chest. The throat itself may be trimmed with thinning scissors as it is rather a tender part. If there are lots of fluffy furnishings some of these may be pulled out as well and this will allow the new coat to come through harder. Trim tail, keeping it thick at the root, tapering it to a point. Strip out the long hairs and finish shaping with serrated scissors. The hair must be cut in the direction of growth to get an even finish, never across as this will leave step marks in the coat. Trim the feet again and check for stones, tar, chewing gum, or mud between the pads.

The time taken for the coat to grow varies slightly from one dog to another but if the puppy fluff has been taken out a new hard coat should be through by the time the puppy is six months old. Once or twice a week go over the body coat and pull out the long ends, lightly thinning the coat. New hair is growing in all the time therefore the dog can be kept in coat continually. If the coat is left too long without attention it will grow long and dead and look extremely shaggy. In this case a complete strip is the only answer, wait for a new coat and then start again. Although this will spoil the appearance temporarily, it will be worth it in the long run. A very hard coated puppy may lack furnishings at this age but they will come later.

Keeping the Coat in Shape
Now the body coat is through and getting thick, the rest of the dog must be put into shape. The head should resemble a

Top left; trimming under the tail (page 49)
Top right; trimming the tail (page 50)
Bottom; stripping the back (page 45)

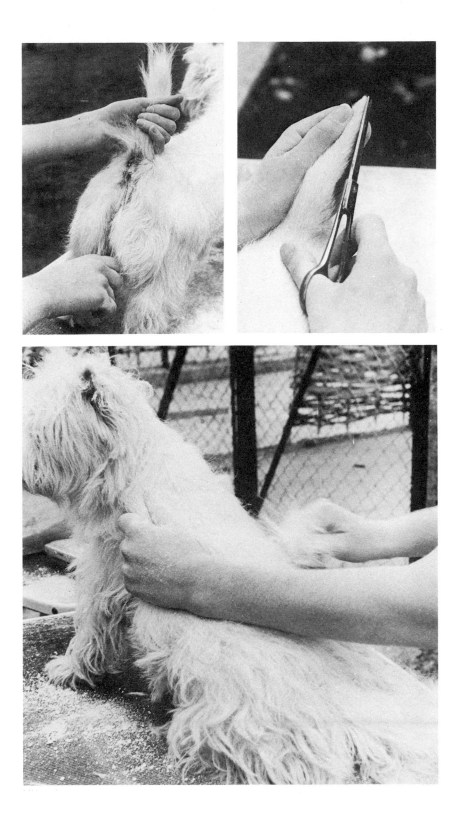

chrysanthemum being nice and round and having thick
furnishings. Place the fingers behind the ears and the
thumbs under the throat thereby making a circle. This
gives you a guide line to shaping the head. Hair behind the
fingers should be stripped out and those in front left to be
shaped into the head. The ears should show about half an
inch above the head furnishings. Trim the hair at the top
of the head between the ears first. This will give you a line
to start the shaping. Very gently, hair by hair, pull out the
long ends all over the head until you have achieved a nice,
round shape.

The hair on the ears should be short, smooth and velvety
with no fringes, and the furnishings left on the lower parts
should blend with the head hair. To keep them tidy, the
ears should be plucked approximately every week. The eyes
should just be seen under heavy eyebrows. The chest hair
is kept fairly short and should be blended in with the longer
hair on the neck and shoulders without any obvious
changes or ridges in the different lengths of hair. You want
to produce a comparatively straight line from the point of
the shoulder down to the toes, the tufty hair on the elbows

A tidy foot (page 49)

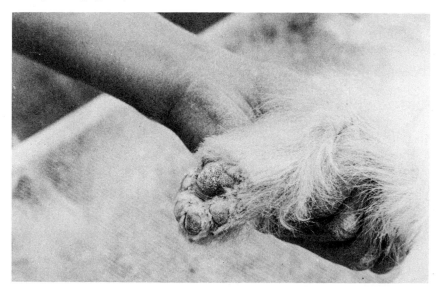

is a tricky part to trim. If you take out too much it will dip
in at the elbows, if you leave too much it will make the dog
look out of line at the elbow, so pull a few hairs, comb into
place and then view. This way you will see when it is just
right. Hair on the back of the front leg is combed outwards
from the leg and any straggling ends are pulled out. This ·
helps the furnishings to thicken up and improves the
appearance. If the dog has a lot of bone, the leg furnishings
can be kept fairly short, but if he is lacking in bone leave
the furnishings as thick as possible. Now the feet: fore feet
are larger than the hind feet. Trim all the hair out from
between the pads but do not trim between the toes. The
feet are supposed to be round so trim them to accentuate
their roundness, and present a clean neat appearance.

Shaping the feet should be done very gradually, it is so
easy to cut too high and emphasize the ankles; the feet are
a continuation of the legs and don't want to look as if they
have been put on afterwards. When trimming front legs
view from front and then from the side as the appearance
should be correct from all angles. The line of the neck must
flow into the back and not be at right angles to it. The
topline must also be level and the coat should be kept at least
two inches long on the back and sides of the body, blending
into longer furnishings. Body furnishings can be too
profuse; if these are excessive they may be shortened as
thin wispy hairs detract from a smart appearance. Use the
stripping knife; the ends may be tipped to improve the outline. Viewed from the rear the hindquarters are quite wide
across the top and continue smoothly down to the feet.
Trimming directly under the tail and approximately
three-quarters of an inch either side of the anus is taken
close with scissors, the rest of the hair should be graduated
towards the outer sides of the quarters until it is blended
in with the longer hairs on the thighs. This is done with
a stripping knife until the dog has a nice flat bottom.
Stifles must be well bent, so with this in mind start
shaping the hindlegs. Don't leave the hair hanging down
to the ground from the stifle, start pulling out the long
wispy ends and remove thick hair on the inside of the
hocks. At the bottom part of the leg the hair is kept quite

short; finish by trimming the feet in the same way as the
front feet were done. Last but by no means least in
importance is the tail, as a badly trimmed tail makes a
considerable difference to the dog's outline. Hair should be
left fairly long on the front, and sides and cut quite closely
at the back. Hair at the base is trimmed with the knife and
nearer the end of the tail on the underside serrated scissors
are used and finally for the tip itself use hair dressing
scissors for the point. Move the scissors round the tail so as

Stripping the chest (page 42)

'Finished effect'–a beautifully trimmed Westie with Catherine Owen

not to have a flat tail. Be careful to let the hair from the
body and quarters merge into the tail so the tail doesn't
look as if it was put on as an afterthought.

Show Points

Rome wasn't built in a day and nor is a show trimming
done in a day. Once the dog is in coat it takes a good month
to get it ready for a show, just a few hairs a day. Brush,
comb, stand the dog, watch it playing and moving. Then
take out the hairs that stick out, and continue in this way.
Incorrect trimming can make a dog with good movement
appear to be a bad mover. Every dog is different, no dog is
perfect, so each one is a new challenge, and one must study
the physical conformation and assess the dog honestly
before you start so that you may enhance all the good
points and minimise the faults.

If the feet turn out, trim the hair tight on the outsides
and leave more on the insides, and if they turn in do the
opposite.

If the dog has a hump or rough back, thin the hair more
drastically on the back than elsewhere but leave sufficient
top coat rather than the soft undercoat.

If the dog dips at the withers, trim the hair shorter
behind the dip and leave the hair as long as possible in the
dip.

For cow hocks (hocks in, feet out), build up between
quarters and feet.

For upright shoulders, leave more hair in at the base of
the neck to flow into the back.

Pet Trimming

It is unnecessary to study the faults and pay as much
attention to detail as in show trimming, but the method is
the same. However, if you would like to keep your dog
smart and still a credit to the breed without quite so much
work you can give it a complete strip or the twice yearly
'do'. Regular grooming will be even more important because
as the coat is longer, food particles will get in the whiskers
and the dog will get shaggy and smelly. The time of the
year the dog is stripped is immaterial; it's when the coat is

ready. In hot weather some people want the coats clipped
down to the skin but this is very cruel as the skin can
easily get sunburnt, causing the dog considerable pain.
'Don't take the coat off or it will catch cold' is the common
saying for the winter; this again is untrue as the undercoat
acts as insulation. A correctly coated Westie should with-
stand all kinds of weather, hot or cold, wet or dry. The top
wiry harsh coat is not shed like smooth-haired breeds,
therefore when the coat is 'blown' – actually a dead coat –
it must be pulled out by the roots. The puppy is usually
about seven months when it is ready for its first complete
strip. Before you start stripping the dog, give it a thorough
grooming, brushing first to loosen any tangles, then comb
through every inch; finish by giving the dog a good chalking brushing the chalk well into the coat. Now you are
ready to start stripping. Make an imaginary line from
behind the ears and back of the head down to the top of the
shoulders down the back to the tail and round to the other
shoulder; all the hair between these two lines is stripped
off. Grip the puppy firmly with the left hand, holding it
slightly above the area to be stripped to keep the skin taut.
If this is not done the skin is pulled with the hair and
causes discomfort to the dog. With the right hand gather a
tuft of hair (topcoat) between the index finger and thumb or
blunt coarse stripping knife and jerk sharply. If the coat is
ready it will come away freely and does not hurt the dog.
Only a few hairs should be pulled at a time and the pull
must always follow the growth of the hairs. At first progress
may seem slow, but speed comes with practice and you will
soon have a 'hole' in the coat leaving the nice soft fluffy
undercoat. The coat is always tougher round the tail and
on the back of the neck, so if you don't want to do the dog
all in one day these are the places to leave for later. Draw
another imaginary line from the base of the ears around the
throat to where the lower jaw joins the neck; you can place
your fingers behind the ears and the thumbs under the
throat thereby making a circle – hair behind the fingers is
stripped out and hair in front left to be shaped into the
head. Strip down the chest to the points of the shoulders.
The legs and head need to be shaped in the same way as a

show dog. The tail will need stripping right out before the
final shaping. If the body furnishings are thick and hang
down, pull out the long ones. Don't pull too far down the
sides as the furnishings start on the side of the rib cage not
underneath. In a fold on the side of each lower lip, there
will usually be a tuft of discoloured hair. Cut this away
with the curved ended scissors taking care not to cut the
lip or other face hair. The dog especially can become very
smelly if he is not kept clean underneath; there is a tuft of
hair in front of the penis which gets wet with urine. This
tuft should be trimmed but not too close as the dog will get
sore. The bitch is apt to wet the long hairs as she 'squats';
this has the same result and can be the source of a strong
'doggy' odour, so it is as well to wash them off from time
to time and, when dry, shake on a little talcum powder.

Bathing
The more the Westie is bathed the dirtier it gets as
shampoos tend to soften the texture of the coat and remove
the natural oils, thus making it more liable to pick up dirt
and dust. However, there are occasions when baths are
necessary – for example, if the dog has external parasites
(fleas, lice, ticks, harvest mites etc.). A medicated bath may
be needed if the dog has a skin irritation. Never give your
Westie a bath without first combing him out to the skin on
every part of his head and body. If you bath the dog in a
matted condition it cannot be rinsed properly and dried
thoroughly and as a result the mats and snarls can
become mildewed (with the accompanying offensive odour)
and the coat will be stained. So groom first, then wash the
dog with tepid water, shampoo (being careful it doesn't go
in his ears and eyes), rinse really well, squeeze out as much
water as possible, rub well with warm towels, and then
comb the hair into place while the dog is drying. If a
medicated bath has been given, the preparation used must
be allowed to dry into the coat to be fully effective. The
dog therefore should be kept in a warm atmosphere to dry,
only the surplus moisture being wrung out and the towel
used as little as possible.
Westies have very sensitive skins; carpets, wool, faulty diet,

vitamin and mineral deficiencies, pollen, fertilisers and insecticides are all irritants to the dog, as are self-inflicted injuries such as nibbling, licking and scratching. The dog can collect fertilizer on the bottoms of its paws out walking, and then only has to scratch its sides before the dog has red sore patches. Eurax lotion and Exmarid lotion are two very good preparations for relieving the irritation. Dogs with skin trouble are rather like children with chicken pox; the spot itches and they scratch it, then the spot gets bigger and so it goes on. If you relieve the dog of the irritation the soreness will soon die down and new hair will appear. In winter the dog undoubtedly spends more time indoors and the dry air of indoor heat doesn't improve the condition of the coat as the skin will tend to be dry and the coat dull. A good balanced diet together with frequent brushing helps to stimulate the secretion of natural oils. A healthy skin is less susceptible to bacterial infection and skin disorders, so keep skin well nourished. Conditioning your dog for a show means preparing a healthy dog inside and outside. Health is the greatest beautifier of all animals. Bitches quite often drop their undercoat after a litter of puppies. If this happens, leave stripping the coat completely until a new undercoat has grown–usually about three months after whelping.

CATHERINE OWEN

Catherine Owen was attending dog shows before she could walk and as her family were connected with terriers it was logical that while she was still at school she was successfully handling her parents' Scottish Terriers at leading shows up and down the country. On leaving school there was no doubt that she would continue as a kennelmaid and her first situation was with a boarding kennels and a Poodle breeder. In 1964 Miss Owen went to the States and worked for a year with a Scottish Terrier Kennels, spending much of the time trimming different breeds for local veterinary surgeons. She gained further experience by travelling to most of the leading shows in the States presenting and handling a number of breeds. Returning to Britain in 1965 Catherine joined her parents in their newly acquired boarding

kennels and Canine Beauty Parlour near St. Albans in Hertford-
shire. She then took over her parents' Westie, Alpinegay Sonata,
and presented and handled this dog, who soon became a champion. Catherine has judged both in Britain and the States, but
much prefers to trim and exhibit her own dogs. This is Catherine's
first attempt at putting her wealth of experience of trimming
into writing, and the diagrams have been done by yet another
West Highland White breeder and exhibitor, Mrs Barbara Hands.

4 Training

BY JOHN HOLMES

The first essential in training is not patience or love of animals as so many people think. And it is not a knowledge of how to make a dog sit, lie down, or take up any other position, as some books would have us believe. The first essential is what I call dog sense – a knowledge of canine mentality – giving one the ability to understand what makes a dog tick.

The reason why the dog is so much easier to train than the cat (which has been domesticated for just as long) is not because it is more intelligent. It is because the dog is a pack animal while the cat prefers a more or less solitary existence. In a pack of dogs there is a very highly developed social order with a leader and followers in a very definite order – top dogs and underdogs, so to speak. One also finds top cats and undercats but there is a vast difference. Whereas the underdogs actually obey and follow their leaders, an undercat simply keeps out of the way of a top cat. The dog's natural instinct is, therefore, to obey a leader, while a cat only wants to please itself, which means that a dog can be made to do certain things we want even when he does not like doing them, while a cat can only be persuaded to do the things it likes doing.

One of the most remarkable features of the domestic dog is the extent to which it still retains the mental characteristics of its wild ancestry. Man has created a larger variety of canine types than in any other domestic species. It is hard to believe that the Pekingese and the Great Dane, the Chihuahua and the Irish Wolfhound all have the same common ancestry. By looking at them one could be excused for saying 'It's impossible!'. But by studying their mental make-up one becomes more and more aware of the similarity in all breeds. Of course different breeds, produced for different jobs, have certain differences in mentality but they are not nearly as great as is generally believed. It is certainly much less than the different opinions of their breeders. Ask a dedicated breeder of *any* breed and he or she will tell you that it is definitely different from *all* other breeds and of course better in every way. And these people

honestly believe what they say for the simple reason that they have never owned any other breed and are so wrapped up in their own that they never even see the breed being judged in the next ring at a dog show. I mention this because I believe that much confusion in training is caused by the idea that each breed has a completely different mentality.

In my time I have trained many dogs for many purposes – film dogs, gun dogs, sheepdogs, guard dogs, working terriers, etc., and I have found that the basic principles of training apply to all dogs of all breeds and indeed to all animals.

The first principle is that by nature the dog wants a leader that it can respect and obey. And he is quite willing, indeed grateful, to be led by a human pack leader. This does not mean that dogs are almost human and it is a dreadful insult to the canine species to suggest that they are. It simply means that we are all animals and many of us are capable of taking on the rôle of pack leader, providing that we are more intelligent and stronger willed than the animal we want to obey us. That many are not is evidenced by the number of disobedient, trouble-making dogs to be seen everywhere.

Here we have a two-way problem. The majority of dogs are what is known as submissive and want to follow a leader but a few are born to be leaders and are known as dominant dogs. Exactly the same happens in the human race and, although we do not usually talk about dominant and submissive people, many readers will know what I mean. The problem usually arises from the fact that a submissive person can rarely train a dominant dog. It is for this reason that a dog will often obey one member of the family and not another. Normally a dog obeys the father first, the mother second and treats young children as equals. But sometimes the dog will obey the mother and take no notice of what the father says. I have invariably found in such cases that the husband obeys the wife too! A dominant person rarely gets the same pleasure from a submissive dog as from a fairly dominant one. Although easy to train to a high standard I get little pleasure from training submissive dogs. All the dogs which stand out in my memory as 'greats' have been dominant, many of them bloody-minded awkward brutes which had been discarded by their previous owners.

This is not a chapter on how to choose a dog but, if you have not already bought one, you should pay particular attention to this point. A person who cannot train one dog may get another *of the same breed* and train it to perfection. Likewise the dog which that person failed to train may go to someone else who will train it quite easily.

The next principle is that dogs do not reason as we do. Here there is considerable difference of opinion. On the one hand there are scientists who say that man is the only animal which reasons. On the other there are people who claim that their dog not only understands every word they say to it but actually talks to them as well, and they carry on regular conversations. Most scientists study dogs under clinical conditions which are quite unnatural. Nothing could be more unnatural than the conditions under which the average domestic dog lives but these are still very different from laboratory conditions, and many pet owners are so preoccupied with turning their dearly beloved into a four-legged human being that they really do believe it does many of the stupid things people do and they never allow it to do any of the clever things which dogs can do.

In my opinion dogs do sometimes reason to a considerable

extent. But we cannot really say to what extent and, as the dog cannot tell us, it is unlikely that we shall ever know. What trainers have learned from experience is that to attempt to train an animal is doomed to failure if it is assumed that it can reason. All training must, therefore, be based on the assumption that *dogs do not reason.*

Dogs learn by association of ideas. They associate certain sounds or sights with pleasure or displeasure. They tend to do the things naturally which result in pleasure and refrain from those which create displeasure. I believe that a dog associates sounds and sights in exactly the same way as we do. All of us can think of a tune, the sound of waves breaking on the seashore, gunfire, a police car siren or one of many other sounds which bring back vivid memories – pleasant or unpleasant – every time we hear them. Like-wise with things we have seen and the same sight and sound may well bring back either pleasant or unpleasant memories, like the sight of a telegram messenger who may bring either good or bad news. The most important thing to remember is that the more pleasant or unpleasant the experience the stronger the association of ideas. To most of us a telegram does not do very much but those who have received tragic news by telegram become apprehensive,

even terrified, of opening another one. In the same way, those who have received glad tidings by telegram will not be apprehensive of receiving one in the future, knowing quite well that it may not bring good news.

The strongest association is built up by fear. If a child gets bitten by a dog it will be excused for having a lifetime fear of dogs. But if a puppy gets kicked by a child people will wonder why it develops a lifelong fear of children and the breeder will be accused of selling a dog with a bad temperament.

First associations are usually much stronger than subsequent ones. If a child has a very unpleasant experience on the first day at school he or she may take a long time to get over it. If this had not occurred until several weeks at school had passed, it might have had little or no effect. People who show dogs know that if a puppy gets a bad fright at its first show it may dislike shows for life. The same experience a year later might have no effect at all.

Another point worth remembering is that dogs, like us, are much more easily upset and with much more lasting effect when they are off colour. An experience which would have little or no effect under normal circumstances can have disastrous results if it happens when a puppy is teething or has a virus infections, or when a bitch is in season, especially for the first time, and in many cases the animal shows no real symptoms of illness.

For training purposes we try to create the association of ideas which we want in the dog and we do it by correction and reward. This means that we try to make it unpleasant for the dog to do the things we don't want him to do and pleasant for him to do the things we do want. The best example of how we should do this is to be seen by studying a bitch with puppies. First of all she supplies them with food from her own mammary glands and later partly digested food which she regurgitates for them. She also licks and caresses them and makes friendly soft noises which fall somewhere between grunting and whining. The puppies, therefore, associate her with food and caressing and every time they see, hear or smell her they rush joyously to her, just as everyone hopes their new puppy

will rush to them; if they feed it, fondle and pet it and make friendly noises to it the chances are that this will happen.

Most people in fact do this, overlooking the fact that the bitch's training does not end there. As the puppies become bigger the bitch, without losing interest in them, does not want to be mauled about by them all the time. Many dog owners put up with that but bitches usually have more sense! So, when the puppies become a bit overbearing the bitch growls at them. Many pups react instinctively to a growl and will stop what they are doing, be it chewing the mother's ear or tail or trying to suckle when there is no milk at the bar, but some bold, dominant pups pay little or no attention. The bitch then repeats her threat and, if there is no response, she will snap at the puppy, often hurting it quite badly by human standards. But she does not hurt it often. Next time the puppy hears an angry growl it associates it with a snap and quickly responds. If it does not, it gets another and another until it *does* respond. When a bitch snaps at a puppy it usually gets a fright and runs away a little distance. But it soon crawls back to be licked and caressed and will soon be happy again.

From this I hope you will realise that far from being unnatural, as some people would have us believe, training is the most natural thing in the world, and the bitch with her puppies (many other animals are similar) is an excellent example of simple and straightforward association of ideas. Once upon a time dogs and children were trained according to these simple principles. We have now become more highly educated and use big words like psychiatrist and psychoanalysis – we even have canine psychologists who have never kept a dog in their lives – and everywhere we find disobedient and unhappy dogs and children.

The dog has a simple straightforward mind. He is highly intelligent but less intelligent than we are. If you are less intelligent than your dog just forget about trying to train him! Most of his senses and instincts are far stronger than ours. He sees as well as we do but, because he is nearer the ground and cannot see what we see, many people say his sight is inferior. He hears many times better than we do but from the shouting at many training classes one could believe that all dogs were deaf. His memory is as good if not better than ours, yet people will marvel at their dog recognising them after a six-week holiday. It would be just as logical to be unable to recognise one's own family – and the dog – after that period. Bearing all the above facts in mind let us now try to apply them to the new puppy you have just bought.

To start with remember that he is only a baby suddenly removed from his mother and probably his brothers and sisters too. At this stage he does not want a leader as much as a comforter to replace his mother. Generally speaking women are much better than men at giving confidence to young animals and it is fortunate that in most households it is the woman who takes the new puppy under her wing. This is not just an idea of my own. The Guide Dogs for the Blind Association employs girls to look after the puppies and to do the initial training while men take over the more advanced training when the dog is old enough to need a leader.

You may have noticed when I was talking about creating associations of ideas I said that we *try* to create those we want and avoid those we do not want. But many wrong associations are built up by ignorance or accident. So far as the new puppy is concerned it is more important to avoid wrong associations than to attempt to create ones we want. Remember what I said about first associations and associations which are created when the animal's resilience is low. A young puppy is much more likely to forget an experience whether pleasant or unpleasant than an older one, but any animal is much more likely to get a bad fright in unfamiliar surroundings than in familiar ones.

Many dogs, I believe, have their temperaments completely ruined the first week they go to a new home as a result of the owner's misguided and often cruel attempts to house train them. A human baby is wrapped in nappies and even an older child is excused of wetting its bed if it is worried or upset, for example when he or she has to stay in a strange house. But a canine baby, which probably has never been in a house and which has been taken from its familiar environment by people it has never seen before, is expected to last all night without making a mistake. When it does it has its nose rubbed in it and probably smacked into the bargain. The owner than says 'I can't understand it. When I brought him home he was so friendly and rushed to greet me. Now he runs and hides every times he sees me'. What would you do if someone treated you like that?

Quite apart from the mental and physical suffering caused to the puppy this method has nothing to commend it. It is highly unlikely that the puppy will associate the punishment with the 'crime' which it could not avoid anyhow. There is, however, every likelihood that it will associate the punishment with the person who administers it and/or the place where it occurred. By persisting in this treatment it is possible to turn a normal bold puppy into a complete nervous wreck in less time than you could believe possible. I know dogs do survive this treatment with no apparent ill effects but they have exceptional temperaments in the first place.

The first object therefore should be to get the puppy to

like you. And you can't make a dog like you any more than you can a person. All you can do is try to be a likeable person in the eyes of the dog by doing the things he likes. A young puppy likes being cuddled, fondled and petted, but not all the time. He wants to run about and play and chew things up. But you don't want him to chew the house to pieces so give him something to play with. Like all young animals he not only wants but needs to sleep. We all know how lack of sleep frays our nerves, making us irritable and bad tempered, but many puppies are kept continually awake because the owner wants to pet or play with them. Children are allowed, even encouraged to run around chasing a puppy often terrifying the life out of it. They give it no peace and one day they get bitten, which serves them right; but it is the puppy which is put down and the children are given another one to torment. If you can't train your children it is unlikely you will train a dog. So, save it a lot of suffering by not having it at all.

These are only a few of the many examples of how unpleasant associations can be created by ignorance and lack of consideration. There can still be accidents. Small puppies, especially friendly ones, are adept at getting under one's feet and it is no good saying that it was his own fault that he got trodden on. A puppy does not reason like that and to him you are just an enormous animal towering above him with a huge foot which causes severe pain when plonked on top of him. There are lots of other things which can happen to puppies like doors being slammed on them and furniture falling on top of them, all of which can have a disastrous and sometimes lasting effect.

The best way to avoid unpleasant experiences to the puppy and at the same time save yourself some unpleasant experiences is to provide a playpen. This can be on the lines of a child's play pen and need not be elaborate or expensive. All that is necessary is an enclosure large enough to give a fair amount of freedom and strong enough to prevent the escape of the puppy in question. As there is so much variation in puppies and the conditions applying to different households I shall not attempt to describe the construction of a play pen. The puppy's bed should be

placed in the pen. There is a wide variety of beds on the
market, such as baskets, ideal for a puppy to chew to
pieces. To the puppy an old tea chest or other box on its
side is just as good if not better, as it is more enclosed. A
board nailed across the front will stop any floor draught
and help to keep in an old piece of blanket or other material
for bedding. Some newspaper should be spread on the floor
of the pen.

The advantage of a play pen should be obvious. While it
not only prevents the creation of many undesirable
associations of ideas, it also prevents the development of
several bad habits. In very few households is there anyone
with the time (even if they had the inclination) to keep a
constant eye on a puppy. If he is in his pen he cannot mess
on the best carpet, chew up the best slippers (they always
choose the best ones), get trodden on or jammed in the door.
Most important of all he won't get on your nerves or you
on his.

If the puppy needs to relieve itself it will use the newspaper which can be picked up without any fuss and bother.
Not that I advocate encouraging the puppy to use it play
pen as a lavatory! The sooner a puppy is house trained the
sooner it is likely to become a pleasant member of the
household but there is rarely any need for drastic methods
so often advocated. And no correction should be applied
until the puppy is happy in its new surroundings and has
complete confidence in its new owner. This may take an
hour with an exceptionally bold puppy brought up in a
house or perhaps two or three days with a less bold puppy
reared in a kennel. An eight-week-old puppy should be
completely confident in three days, if not there is something
wrong either with the pup or the new home. Generally
speaking the older a dog is the longer it will take to settle
down and the more effect its previous upbringing will have.
For instance, a pup reared from eight weeks in a home with
children can at six months go to another home with
children and settle down right away, but the same pup if
reared in a home with a quiet elderly couple, or in kennels
with a lot of other dogs, might never get over the shock of
a house full of noisy children. We have found that one of

the worst ages to change a puppy's environment is between four and five months old when it is teething.

To return to the question of house training few people realise that the average puppy wants to be clean in its own living quarters. All animals born in nests learn at quite an early age to go out of the nest to relieve themselves, thereby keeping their living quarters clean. The object should be to develop this instinct which can usually be done without any correction at all and certainly without the brutal treatment so often administered.

The first essential is an observant owner. Because of its instinct to be clean nearly every puppy will show symptoms of wanting to relieve itself. Unfortunately few owners recognise these symptoms and expect the puppy to ask to go out by whimpering or even barking. The most usual symptom is when the puppy simply starts looking around and probably sniffing the floor. When this happens take him out, wait until he has done what he has to do, praise him well and bring him back in. Don't just push him out and shut the door. He may well have decided that the door mat was the ideal place for his purpose and wait on the doorstep until the door opens, when he will come in and do what he intended doing exactly where he intended doing it. If you do catch a puppy actually in the act of squatting down pick him up firmly by the scruff say 'No' or 'Bad boy' in a corrective tone (the equivalent of his mother's growl) and take him out. To a young puppy this is *very* severe correction and should be done quietly without any shouting or flapping of folded newspapers so often recommended.

The important thing is to catch the puppy in the act and this rule applies to all training. Correction after the event (even seconds after) is unlikely to do any good and more than likely to do a great deal of harm. Remember that we are trying to work on the dog's mind and not his body and he will associate correction with what is on his mind at the time. For instance if a dog is corrected when he is looking at a cat with the obvious intention of chasing it that should be very effective. If he is corrected as he is chasing the cat that should be effective too. But if he chases a cat up a tree and you correct him when he returns

to you, you will have corrected him for coming back, not
for chasing cats. In this way many dogs are taught by their
owners *not* to come back when called – and they still
chase cats!

In the same way many puppies become afraid of owners
who leave them alone for hours then return and punish
them for wetting on the floor – which the poor little
blighter could not avoid anyway. 'Of course he knows,' they
say. 'Just see how guilty he looks.' But he does not look
guilty at all, he simply looks afraid and with very good
reason. You can prove this for yourself by scolding any
reasonably sensitive dog when it has done nothing wrong
and it will immediately look 'guilty' through fear or
apprehension.

If one has to leave a puppy for a long period, put him in
his play pen and of course he can sleep in it at night. All
one has to do then is pick up the soiled newspaper. As he
gets older he should learn to wait until he is let out and
should be able to do so. A puppy accustomed to newspaper
will sometimes prefer to use it in preference to going out.
If you take it up and keep an eye on him you should notice
when he goes looking for it and take that as a signal to
let him out.

Our own dogs are never house trained in the generally
accepted sense but simply encouraged to develop their
instinct to be clean. Some live in the house and some in
kennels and it is rare indeed for an adult to make a mistake
in either. They work in studios, live with us in a motor
caravan and often stay in hotels and the only problem we
ever have is when a director wants a dog to lift its leg in
the studio! Having been encouraged to be clean very few of
our dogs will do this indoors but will readily oblige outside
on the studio lot.

Dog training cannot be divided into compartments and it
is useless deciding to spend a fortnight on one exercise and
then a fortnight on another. All training must synchronise
and a lot of it has to take place simultaneously. There are
however, certain 'exercises' which must be learnt before
going on to other exercises. These are the basic exercises
and the important point about them is that once the

teacher and the pupil understand them thoroughly they can go on to more advanced exercises at any time – even after a lapse of several years. Space being limited I intend to deal only with the basic exercises. By the time you have mastered them I hope you will be keen enough on training to buy a book and proceed to more advanced training.

My reason for starting with house training is not because it is more important than other exercise or because it should be taught first. Indeed it is the only exercise which is of no benefit to anyone except the owner – or his friends who visit his house – which is probably why the average owner is so much keener on house training than on teaching the dog not to bite the postman! And that is why I started with it – because it is the first thing most people want to know about. There is actually another reason for starting house training soon after a puppy goes to a new home. A puppy with a strong instinct to be clean will soon choose a secluded spot as a 'loo' and will always go there. If that happens to be at the bottom of the garden it's fine. But if it happens to be behind the piano or the couch in the best room that's not so funny. And if an idea like that (based on an instinct) is allowed to develop it can be very difficult to change. All training must endeavour to create good habits and prevent bad ones.

One good habit which the puppy should learn right from the start is to come when called. In spite of everything you believe or have been told about dogs that 'understand every word said to him' dogs do not in fact, understand any words at all. They simply recognise sounds (far more accurately than we do) and they associate these sounds with certain actions. If your dog gets excited when you mention 'Walk' it is simply because he associates that sound (not a word to him) with going for a walk. Instead of recognising that simple fact dog owners resort to spelling the word. Very soon the dog associates the sounds W-A-L-K with going for a walk and his owners think he has learnt to spell!

At this stage we are mainly concerned with encouraging the puppy to come to us in response to a particular sound. The sound is usually the dog's name and where there are a lot of dogs, such as we keep, it is important that each and

every one responds to its own name and to no other. But we do not go around repeating a dog's name over and over again for no reason at all. We use the dog's name when we want him to come to us – and if we don't want him we don't call him. The average owner, however, appears unable to desist from repeating the puppy's name every time he sees it. Not only that – the whole family, friends and neighbours will want to have cosy chats with any new puppy repeating its name over and over again in the process. Any new puppy we get will come to us in response to its name within a day or two but the average puppy hears its name so much that it completely ignores the sound just as it does the sound of the radio or television.

Constantly repeated sounds without association become ignored. For that reason it is often advisable to teach a dog to come to you in response to a different sound altogether like 'here' or 'come'. The word matters not and it is just as easy to teach a dog to come by saying 'go' as by saying 'come'. What does matter is that you always use the same command and use it in the right tone of voice. As I said earlier, a puppy instinctively cowers or even runs away at the sound of its mother's growl and will rush to greet her when she makes her soft welcoming noise, which is almost inaudible to human ears. The ability to change the tone of voice is vital in training and is one of the gifts which divides successful trainers into successful and unsuccessful. Don't confuse tone with volume. It is never necessary to shout at a puppy in the confines of its own house.

Now we come to the big question. How do you teach this charming puppy to rush to you in joyous bounds every time you call it? To start with you want to persuade rather than try to make it come. Later you may have to make him (he may have lost some of his charm by then!) but try persuasion first.

Obviously you should start by calling the puppy in a nice friendly persuasive tone of voice, never in a harsh correcting tone. If you stand straight up he is likely to stand back staring at the great thing towering above him but if you squat down he should come up to you even if you do not ask him.

A timid puppy will move away every time you move towards him but is almost certain to come nearer if you move away from him.

An outstretched hand with moving fingers will attract nearly any puppy, and many adult dogs, while the same hand with fist clenched will be ignored. There is a general belief that one should always present the back of the hand to a strange dog. Working with dogs as I do in close contact with a great variety of self-styled dog lovers I find the efforts to carry out this exercise as amusing as it is unsuccessful.

Perhaps the commonest of all mistakes which people make in approaching a strange dog (and that includes a new puppy) is to stare at it. The only animal which likes its friends to look it 'straight in the eye' is the human being. Other animals do this only if they are afraid of each other or are about to attack. Watch two dogs meeting. If they look straight at each other you can expect a fight but if they approach shoulder to shoulder and walk stiffly round and round each other they will end up on friendly terms; so never stare at a new puppy when you are trying to get on friendly terms.

Now you are out in the garden with your pride and joy and you want him to come when called. He is probably sniffing around the gatepost or digging up the flower bed. Don't call him – for the simple and obvious reason that he won't come anyhow! An untrained puppy will do the thing which provides, or is likely to provide, the greatest pleasure at the time. Anyone who thinks that his voice is more attractive to a puppy than a hole in the ground or a smell on a gatepost has got the puppy's priorities wrong. Wait until the puppy appears to have nothing important to do and call it then. The best time is usually when he happens to be coming to you anyhow. Crouch down, hand extended, and call the puppy in a friendly persuasive tone. When he reaches you make a great fuss, fondle him and possibly offer a reward in the form of food. Do this several times when the puppy is sure to come and he will soon associate the sound of his name with the reward of food and/or petting. He will then have this association of ideas to strengthen the natural inclination to go to a friendly voice or hand. In most cases this combination will soon be strong enough to induce the puppy to leave the hole he is digging or the smell he is sniffing.

The mistake most people make is in never calling the puppy unless he is doing something they don't want him to do – which is usually something he *does* want to do. Every time you call a puppy and he obeys you (even if he happened to be coming anyhow) you have gone a step forward. Every time you call him and he disobeys you you have gone a step back. And if you persist in calling him when he is certain to disobey you, you will actually teach him *not* to come when called. Whatever you do, never, under any circumstances, scold or correct a dog in any way when it comes to you – no matter how much you feel like murdering it!

Now we have a puppy which comes to you in response to reward alone. But he will only do so if the reward is better than the alternative – and dog's lives, like ours, are made up of alternatives. A puppy will probably find food and petting more rewarding than aimlessly digging a hole or sniffing round a gatepost. But if the hole leads to a stinking old bone previously buried there or, when the dog is a bit older, a bitch in season has been around the gatepost, cooing voice, outstretched hand and pocketfuls of titbits may prove to be a poor alternative. We must then resort to correction as well as reward to build up the association we want. It should be noted that correction is only resorted to when reward has failed.

Our puppy is back in the same hole and you call him as before. But this is a much more interesting hole and, if the puppy responds at all, it is merely to look up as if saying 'Hang on a minute, I'm busy'. Here we have a situation

where it is very easy to correct the puppy as he is doing
the wrong thing and you should always take advantage of
such opportunities. You have *asked* the puppy to come by
calling his name in a nice friendly tone and he has refused.
Call his name again, this time *telling* him to come in a very
firm tone. It is possible that the puppy may respond to this
change of tone. If so, change your tone of voice and whole
attitude completely, and reward him with enthusiasm. If he
does not respond pick up a handful of earth or small gravel
and call him again even more harshly. If he does not
respond this time throw the earth or gravel at him. As this
'hail' descends on him from heaven he will almost certainly
get a fright and look round for a protector – that's you!
Call him to you, make a great fuss of him and do all you
can to console him in his misfortune. The object is to get
him to associate the harsh tone of voice with something
nasty out of the blue. He must not know that you threw it
and, if you do it properly, it is almost certain that next
time he hears that harsh tone he will anticipate another
'hailstorm' and rush to you for protection – which you
must always provide.

Never allow a puppy to run loose in a strange place until
he will come to you every time you call him in the house or
garden. Even then, you may find that when he sees another
dog in the park he rushes off. I cannot over-emphasise the
importance of nipping this habit in the bud and the best
way for the novice is probably by using a check cord –
about thirty feet of light cord attached to a dog's collar at
one end with the other end in your hand. Let the puppy
rush off and, as he nears the end of the cord call his name
in a harsh tone. This time, instead of the handful of earth,
the jerk on the check cord will provide the correction. He
will probably do a somersault but don't worry. This method
has been used by generations of gun dog trainers and I
have never heard of a dog hurting himself. As he recovers
from the jerk call him in a nice friendly tone and, when he
reaches you, reward him lavishly. Never drag him to you.
The line should be used as a means of correction when the
dog tries to run away but you should encourage him to you
by reward.

This method of training should naturally never be carried out until the dog is on a collar and lead and it is unlikely that a puppy will run after other dogs until he is about six months old. He will have to learn to go on a collar and lead before you take him out in public, and the place to teach him is not on the street or in the park but in his own garden or even indoors. Remember that a lead should never be regarded as a means of making a dog go with you but merely as a means of preventing him going too far away. Never put a collar and lead on a puppy until he will follow you without one.

There is a lot of argument about the best type of collar. Generally speaking, an ordinary buckled leather collar is as good as any for a puppy to start with. The puppy can be allowed to wear one and become quite familiar with it before the lead is put on. Start with a long lead and use it only to stop the puppy. Encourage him to come with you by rewarding him in the ways I have already described. Providing he will follow you without a lead (even if you do carry food in your pocket) he should soon follow you with one. It is more a question of familiarisation than actual training.

The usual problem is not how to get a puppy to go on a lead but how to stop him pulling once he has become familiar with it.

Here again this should be stopped before it becomes a habit, which is easier to prevent than to cure. It is import-ant that when the puppy pulls you do not pull against him. Correct him for pulling with a sharp jerk on the lead and when he comes back to you in response, praise him well. Obviously you cannot jerk a dog on a short lead. For training a lead should be three or four feet long, pliable (we now use nylon web leads almost entirely), with a strong clip. If the puppy pulls, let the lead go suddenly and, before he has regained his balance, give him a sharp jerk. With a young puppy quite a small jerk will suffice, but it requires a considerable amount of skill and strength to cure an adult dog of pulling. There is little pleasure in taking out a dog which constantly pulls so, for your own sake as well as the dog's, don't let the habit develop.

Sally Anne Thompson

If, in spite of your efforts, the puppy is pulling by the time he is six months old I would suggest taking him to a local training class. I have mixed feelings about training classes where one often finds the blind leading the blind – not very successfully either! I get a great many cries for help from dog owners and almost all of them have already attended training classes! Some of the advice given by self-styled experts is quite frightening. I have met many sensitive dogs with temperaments completely ruined by classes.

On the other hand I know many dogs and owners who have benefited beyond belief. Like many other successful trainers, I started by going to classes. It really all depends on the instructor who in this country (not in America) gives his services free. Unfortunately free advice is often worth just what it costs. My advice is to go along to a training class (the Kennel Club will give you a list of those in your area) without your dog and see whether dogs which have been attending for some time behave in the way you want your dog to behave.

You now have a puppy which is clean in the house, comes when you call it (and stays with you) and walks on a loose lead. The other important exercise to make him a pleasure rather than a nuisance is that he stays where he is told without bringing complaints from the neighbours. Here we must go right back to the beginning with the puppy in the play pen. If, when you leave him, he cries to get out and you take him out you will be rewarding him for crying. It is incredible how quickly a young puppy will learn that whenever it wants attention all it has to do is howl. The longer you stay with a puppy coddling and consoling him the longer he will whine or howl when you leave him. If you go away and leave him alone he will probably howl for a bit and then settle down and go to sleep. A puppy accustomed from the start to being left alone in his play pen is unlikely to create any problems when you come to leave him in the car or any other strange place.

If he does persist in howling or barking when left alone, put him in his pen or just shut him in a room and go away. Stop when you get out of sight and wait for the noise to start. When it does, go back quietly. The puppy won't hear you when he is making a noise but he will whenever he stops, so you must stop and wait until he starts again. The idea is to get right up to the door while he is actually making a noise, then open it suddenly (which will surprise him anyhow) grab hold of him and scold him severely. Now start all over again, and if he makes a noise repeat the whole process. It is unlikely that he will make a noise this time so wait a few moments (don't tempt Providence by waiting too long) and go back to him again. This time make a great fuss to reward him for being quiet.

The usual mistake people make is unintentionally rewarding the dog for making a noise. The say 'Now, now, be a good boy. Don't make a noise', or 'It's all right, Mummy's here. No need to cry about it', and they say it all in the most soothing and rewarding tone possible. Having been rewarded by tone of voice (probably by gentle stroking too) for barking or whining the dog naturally does it again, and again, and again for as long as he is rewarded. It is interesting to note that bad tempered owners never have problems of this sort. They don't wonder what to do or read books on the subject. The dog irritates them by making a noise and, as it is actually barking, is told in no uncertain terms to 'Shut up'. If it doesn't, it gets a hefty clout on the ear and next time it hears 'Shut up' it shuts up! That is not how I train dogs or believe that dogs should be trained but it is effective.

Your pup should now be clean in the house, come when called (at any time and in any place) and be quiet when left on his own. And that is more than can be said for many of the dogs working in the Obedience Championships at Crufts! If you do aspire to more advanced training (and I hope some of my readers will) there are several books on the subject and plenty of people willing to offer advice.

JOHN HOLMES

An animal man if ever there was one, John Holmes was born and brought up on a farm in Scotland, and is the son of a famous breeder and exhibitor of Clydesdale horses and a judge of horses and cattle. As a boy he kept terriers who earned their keep by keeping the farm free of vermin. As an encore the terrier team entertained the farm workers and locals with a variety of party tricks. Later he graduated to training sheep- and cattle-dogs, using them for real work; he drove sheep ten miles to Perth market once a week, summer and winter, for a number of years.

He bought his first Corgi, Nippy of Drumharrow, in 1933 for two guineas, and later owned many famous Corgis. Mr Holmes took up obedience training after the war and in 1950 won the Junior Stakes at the ASPADS Trials; he then started training difficult and disobedient dogs for other people, and in no time at all became a prominent figure with a nationwide reputation.

In his own words, at this point he really began to learn about dogs and, more important, dog people. He ran dog training classes at Henley on Thames, and among other successes the instructor married his 'star pupil'. Together, Mr and Mrs Holmes built up a team of dogs who gave displays all over the British Isles – a mongrel from the team started his film career in 'Knave of Hearts'. This was quickly followed by a television series of dog programmes, 'Your Dog and Mine', for which John supplied the performers. Since then he has handled all sorts of other animals, including rats, on hundreds of films, television plays and commercials, and has appeared in numerous documentaries and discussion programmes on television. His film, 'A Tale of Two Puppies', was networked over all regions around Christmas 1970, and he has also made a seven-episode series for Southern Television called 'Training the Family Dog' based on his book *The Family Dog* (now in its fifth edition). Other books by John Holmes include *The Farmer's Dog* (about training sheep- and cattle-dogs) and *Obedience Training for Dogs*.

J.C.

5 Training for the Show Ring
BY CATHERINE OWEN

A pleasant living environment should not be considered a substitute for loving, personal contact with your puppy. The two should be inter-related to establish the puppy's disposition and behaviour patterns. Puppies should be played with and handled from an early age as attention in the early weeks proves priceless in developing their characters and prevents them from being hand shy. Half the puppy's disposition is inborn and half is made. It is important that the puppy is fearless of the everyday noises of life, radios, traffic, children screaming and so on. It is not too soon when they first leave the dam at six weeks for you to get down on your knees and pose the puppy on the floor by pushing the tail into an upright position and lifting the head. At eight weeks the puppy should be beginning to learn how to stand on the table and grooming sessions are a good time to practise this. Be careful while lifting the puppy that it does not wriggle out of your arms onto the floor and that once you have it on the table it does not attempt to leap off. The puppy must be restrained all the time as it will seem to have no sense of danger.

Collar and lead training is the next step. Always use a small thin lightweight collar and lead and make sure that it is tight enough so that it cannot be slipped over the head, but not too tight so that it will choke the puppy. Make sure that the lead is under the chin and not on top of the neck or else the collar can be pulled off. The puppy should be taught to walk on both a loose and a tight lead and also on your left and right side as there will be occasions when you will need to walk your dog on the right side. Some enjoy learning and have a great desire to please whereas others are naughty and stubborn. They are extremely independent and sulk, fight, pull, tug, buck, or scratch, but with practice, patience, perseverance and determination on your part it will come. On the whole Westies are an easy breed to train to the lead.

As soon as the puppy is inoculated, road exercise can begin. It is best to take an older dog with the puppy to give it confidence, as the strange noises of cars can be very bewildering and frightening. Lessons should be short

but frequent, and exercise should be restricted. Puppies that run around all day tend to be long in back, and those that are allowed up and down steps tend to be out at the elbow. Before the puppy starts teething it should be accustomed to having its mouth examined. When they do start to change teeth the gums become quite sore so occasionally examine the mouth, very gently, to make sure the teeth are coming through all right. It is beneficial to get the puppy accustomed to being handled by strangers, preferably someone who knows how to handle a show dog, feeling the puppy all over and opening its mouth.

Training should be fun at all times and the best instrument to help you is your voice which should be used to praise and encourage your puppy at all times. The more you speak to it the more responsive the puppy will become. If you have a ringcraft club locally it's worth attending them as training classes introduce your puppy to actual show conditions. As it's like a play show, they can socialise and meet strangers and dogs of all shapes and sizes. It may also involve a car journey which is good practise. You can train the puppy to walk, stand with its tail up and look alert and teach it to show itself off to the best advantage. Temperament is paramount in importance. The puppy should be bold so that it carries itself well in the show ring, but not unduly aggressive. A happy dog is a sign of a well-balanced disposition. Try to avoid letting a puppy be frightened as it will never forget. If a puppy has been spoilt it will probably be very excitable and under these circumstances a short, sharp shaking is more effective than any number of smacks. Remember, start training your puppy the day before it starts training you. If trained correctly there is nothing better than a well-mannered Westie because along with all their other traits they are well behaved with children.

Why do we have dog shows? Show wins bring several advantages; puppies from one or both parents that are show winners fetch higher prices and are sold more readily. Dogs at stud command higher fees if they themselves have won at shows or sired show winners. A show is a breeder's 'shop window', a good dog, happy and well presented, will sell your stock to the public. Most of all the honour of

winning and the pride in one's dog is a great reward to its
owner. To breed, own, prepare and handle is an even
greater thrill. Do not be reluctant to admit that you are a
novice exhibitor; go to a show dogless first to see and learn
all you can, ask questions but, please, not when an
exhibitor is busy preparing a dog for the ring.

6 Breeding

BY BETTY PENN-BULL

There is an old theory that every bitch should have a litter, but there seems to be no evidence to support this, so unless there is a definite desire to breed, the certainty of placing the resulting puppies satisfactorily, and the ability to provide the necessary care and attention, it is not advisable to embark on mating a bitch.

My opinion is that a bitch is best bred from either regularly or not at all, and that the single, so-called 'therapeutic' litter may well unsettle her, awakening the maternal and breeding instincts which are then subsequently thwarted if she is not allowed further puppies.

I have known many maiden bitches which have lived healthy lives into ripe old age, and I do not advise anyone to mate a bitch unless the puppies are really wanted. Never do so 'for her sake' and risk bringing puppies into the world for which it may be impossible to find good and suitable homes.

There are new opinions these days in regard to spaying bitches, and this now seems to be more acceptable than it used to be. But it is important that a bitch is fully developed before this is done, and she should have had at least one season in order to have reached complete maturity. Guide Dogs For The Blind use spayed bitches almost without exception, and this has not been found to affect their disposition, health, well-being or ability to work adversely.

Small breeds are usually easily controlled when in season, but with the larger ones, or where premises are not completely secure from invasion by trespassing dogs, spaying is certainly preferable to mis-mating and a subsequent unwanted litter.

Bitches used for breeding should conform to certain standards physically and mentally, and those falling short of these requirements should be discarded. They should be sound and healthy, of good type and conformation, and free from structural, organic or hereditary defects. In addition they should be of good temperament; nervous or bad-tempered stock should not be bred from. People sometimes appear to have the wrong ideas about breeding and I have heard remarks like, 'She is so nervous and excitable, I think a litter will steady her'; 'She keeps getting skin trouble, I hope having puppies will help to clear it up'. I feel this argument should be in reverse. Are these dogs suitable to be bred from? Do we want half a dozen more with poor temperaments or with some physical disability? If the answer is that we do not, then the simple solution is not to breed from such stock, and they should be excluded from one's breeding programme. The possibility of benefiting the parent at the expense of the unborn young is a wrong concept.

Before being mated the bitch should be in top condition and perfect health. She should be well nourished on a properly balanced diet with ample protein, but it is preferable if she is a little on the lean side rather than slightly too fat.

Bitches normally come into season for the first time at about nine months of age, and thereafter at six monthly intervals. But there may be some variation in these times and this is not necessarily an indication of any abnormality. Small dogs in particular may have their first heat as young as seven or eight months of age, while larger ones may be a year old or even older. The cycle may vary too, and occasionally a bitch will go twelve months between seasons, while with some of the smaller breeds it may occur again after only four months' intervals. But if a bitch has three seasons in a year, one of these will not be fertile. Usually, after a litter the cycle adjusts and the times revert to the normal six months. When a bitch is due in season she should be tested each day with a swab of cotton wool pressed to the vulva to check for the first sign of colour. She can then be observed, and the pattern of her season noted.

As a rule, dogs tend to sniff around a bitch and show interest before the season actually starts, and this is often an indication that it is pending. But once the colour appears most dogs leave a bitch severely alone during the early period and I do not usually find it necessary to segregate her for at least six or seven days. After this time she must be carefully isolated.

Colour usually continues for about nine or ten days and then it gradually begins to fade, and by about twelve days, which is normally the height of the season, there is either just a pinkish tinge or it is practically colourless. As a rule the heat lasts for three weeks and the bitch must be kept isolated until the end of this period whether mated or not.

With some of the smaller breeds there is a more rapid cycle, the colour fades sooner and the bitch may be ready at eight or nine days, and the season completely over in fourteen or fifteen days. Some of the larger breeds may not be ready to mate until fourteen to sixteen days or even later, and their season may last twenty-four days, or occasionally even longer, so each bitch must be studied individually. It is important to note details of the first season as this can be helpful on subsequent occasions if a mating is intended.

With the smaller breeds the second season is a suitable time for mating, and this usually occurs at about fifteen months of age. But if a bitch is being shown, or it is not convenient, she can be left until later. It is advisable when possible to have her first litter by about three years of age while the frame is still elastic and has not hardened too much.

If a bitch is bred from regularly but has not been over-bred, I have known a number to continue having success-ful litters up to eight years of age. But it is important that she is maintained in good condition and receives the right care and attention.

It is not possible to generalise in regard to the frequency with which one can mate a bitch as each case must be assessed on its own merits.

As a rough guide the larger breeds which also tend to have larger litters may need a longer time between litters. With the smaller breeds one can often have two litters in succession and then miss a season without putting an undue strain on the bitch. But other factors come into

Sally Anne Thompson

account too, particularly the number of puppies produced and reared. If a bitch had seven or eight and reared all I would rest her a year before the next litter. But if she had only three or four I would consider mating her at her next heat. This would apply during the prime of her life, between two and six years old, but after six years of age I would not breed from her more than once a year.

Other factors must be considered too, such as her general health, condition and activity and whether she is an easy whelper. Some dogs of seven are like four-year-olds, and others are like ten-year-olds, so all these matters must be taken into account.

Arrangements should be made well in advance with the owner of the selected stud dog, and it is customary for her to visit him. A provisional date should be fixed as soon as she starts in season which can be varied later if necessary.

If the bitch is sent by rail she should be despatched two or three days before the height of her season and in consultation with the owner of the dog. She should be sent in a secure and comfortable box, properly labelled and with careful arrangements for her collection.

If she is taken personally which is preferable whenever possible, it is important the timing is correct to ensure maximum prospects of a successful outcome, and this entails the careful assessment of the vital factors of the timing, colour and her reactions. On arrival the bitch should be allowed a free run to relieve herself, to stretch her legs and to settle down a little after her journey, before being introduced to the dog. The actual mating procedure is dealt with under the section concerned with the stud dog.

After mating, the bitch must be kept segregated until the completion of her season, and she can then resume her normal life.

Care of the Bitch In Whelp
The bitch in whelp should be well cared for, but not coddled. For the first few weeks she may carry on with her ordinary routine providing this does not entail any excessive exertion. But she will be all the better for plenty of freedom and exercise, interspersed with adequate rest periods. She should not be allowed to get cold or wet, and should also be protected from excessive heat.

During the last few weeks several short walks are preferable to one long one, but she should be encouraged to keep active with gentle exercise until the end, although avoiding anything unduly strenuous. She should have as much liberty as possible and should not be closely confined except for minimal periods.

Feeding the in-whelp bitch may vary to some degree. With the small breeds, and with some which are not always easy whelpers, great care must be taken not to over-feed, and the aim is to produce small, strong puppies at birth, as larger ones may well be the cause of trouble at whelping time.

I feed as usual for the first six weeks, but I do ensure there is an ample meat ration, plus a limited amount of biscuit and raw or cooked vegetables. I give two equal meals for the last three weeks, increasing the meat allowance but decreasing the starch to a minimum. I give cod liver oil daily, but this is the only additive my bitches in whelp receive as they are a breed which are not always easy whelpers, so I ration them carefully: I do not add calcium or bone meal, or give milk or eggs or other extras.

But with many other breeds, and particularly the larger ones, it will be advisable to step up the rations after mating, and probably to provide various additives too, as this particular problem of whelping does not apply in all cases.

The big breeds usually have larger litters and the puppies are proportionately smaller at birth in relation to the size of the dam. So within certain limits the breeder must be

guided by the needs of the individual bitch in deciding on the correct policy.

I give a small teaspoonful of liquid paraffin daily during the last week. I also give the bitch a thorough grooming and overhaul several days before the litter is due. This consists of a good brushing and combing into every corner. She is then sponged over with a cloth wrung out in weak Dettol and warm water, paying particular attention to the feet, under the body, the head, between the legs and under the tail. The anal gland is checked and cleared if necessary. The eyes and ears are examined and treated if required, and the mouth and teeth are inspected and cleaned if necessary.

Any excessive hair round feet, tummy and other parts may be tidied up if desired, but although I have a breed with furnishings I do not remove them from my bitches. Some breeders do, and this is a matter for the individual to decide.

The Whelping Quarters

The bitch should be introduced to the place where she is to whelp some days before the event, so she feels settled and relaxed there. This should be a quiet room or building, or an enclosed pen where she has privacy and is not worried by other dogs or by children or strangers.

The whelping box should be placed here, and it should be roomy enough for her to lie full length and still allow a margin of space beyond this. It should be raised on low slats to allow air to circulate beneath the base. There should be a removable board to slot into the front, but this should be taken out before whelping to avoid any risk of injury when the bitch goes in and out of the box. The sides of the box should be high enough to protect the bitch and puppies from draughts and a removable lid is an advantage.

A crush barrier should be provided which can be inserted into the box, with a clearance of two or more inches from the ground, and two or more inches from the sides of the box, according to the size of the dog, to avoid the possibility of the puppies being pressed behind the dam, and perhaps suffocated. This is similar to the pig-rail used for

farrowing sows and provides a safe alley-way while the puppies are small. This barrier should not be put into position until after the bitch has finished whelping and it can be removed when the puppies are two or three weeks old, when they require more room and will be stronger.

I use an infra-red lamp for my litters and this is positioned across one corner of the box, so there is a warm spot for the puppies, but the opposite corner is cool if the dam prefers to lie there.

My whelping box has vinyl on the floor and this is then covered with several layers of newspaper and finally a thick blanket for the bitch and litter.

The Whelping

Bitches carry their young for sixty-three days, but this is subject to some variation. It is quite usual for a bitch to whelp three days early, while some of the smaller breeds may have their puppies five days before time. Puppies born more than five days early have a limited chance of survival. Some bitches may go overtime, but if this extends more than two or three days there is some cause for concern and there may be trouble ahead.

The first indication that whelping may be imminent is a drop in temperature which will fall below 100° (normal temperature in the dog is 101·4°). This may occur two or three days before the actual whelping, but when the temperature drops to 98° or 97° the whelping will generally occur within twenty-four hours.

The preliminary signs are restlessness, trembling, yawning, panting, bed-making, and possibly vomiting. Food is usually refused, and there is often a desire to pass water frequently.

All these symptoms may be present, or only some, and they may last for some hours, or even intermittently for a full day or more. But the whelping as such does not really commence until the contractions begin, so until that time it is a matter of waiting for further developments.

If there is a rise in temperature or a black or green discharge, trouble is indicated and veterinary advice must be sought without delay.

But if all appears normal do not interfere unnecessarily, but allow the bitch the opportunity to whelp. Some are

slower than others, and it sometimes pays to be patient
providing there are no abnormal symptoms.

Many bitches like the comfort of their owner's presence
at this time, and a reassuring word and a little fondling
will encourage them. Firm, but gentle stroking down the
back is sometimes helpful in stimulating the contractions.

The bitch should not be fussed or agitated and the owner
should remain calm and cheerful. The bitch can be offered
glucose and milk or glucose and water from time to time,
or she may be given a little brandy or whisky, but she
should not have any solid food during whelping as this may
cause vomiting.

The first puppy may appear quite quickly once the contractions start, or it may not come for two or three hours,
or even more in some cases, as some bitches are much
slower than others.

It is sometimes difficult to decide at what stage assistance
should be given, and if an owner is a complete novice it is
helpful to have an experienced breeder available who can
advise in the event of any queries or difficulties or suggest
when professional help is necessary.

The puppy should arrive head first, contained in its sac
and with the afterbirth attached, and the dam should
quickly release the puppy, cleaning it thoroughly and
eating the afterbirth. But some bitches, particularly
maidens, are slow at freeing the puppy's head, and in this
case the breeder must do so without delay or fluid will get
into the puppy's lungs and this may be fatal. The bitch
should then be encouraged to lick and massage the puppy.
If it is slow in breathing it should be rubbed and shaken
and any fluid drawn from the nose and mouth; warmth is
very important in helping to revive it.

The flat-nosed breeds are not usually able to attend to
their newly-born whelps, and the attendant must be
prepared to assist them by removing the puppy from the
bag and severing the cord. The puppy should then be
offered to the dam for her to clean and lick. If several
puppies are born in rapid succession it may be advisable to
remove some of the earlier ones temporarily and place them
in a warm box away from the dam until the whelping is

completed so that the newer arrivals can receive more attention, and the earlier ones do not get cold and neglected. But if this upsets the dam they must be left with her and endeavours made to keep them warm and dry. I use thick newspapers for the whelping and old sacks or blankets, and I put in more paper or old towels as we go along, to try and keep the bed as clean and dry as possible.

When the whelping is finished one person should take the bitch out to make herself comfortable. Meanwhile, a second person should gently lift out the puppies, then remove the soiled bedding, wipe round the box and put in fresh paper and a clean blanket. The anti-crush frame should then be inserted, the front board slotted in and the puppies replaced. The dam should then be allowed back, to find everything ship-shape, thus avoiding her being agitated by a lot of commotion going on around her.

She should be offered a warm drink and then left quietly to rest for a few hours, although it is generally wise to keep an unobtrusive eye on her to make sure all is well. I leave a small light for the first few days as I prefer a dull emitter lamp over the bed.

Post-Natal Care and Feeding
For the first few days after whelping it is important to check the bitch's mammary glands regularly. Run the hands lightly over all her teats and these should be soft and yielding. If one or more are hard and congested this indicates the puppies are not suckling from these, and this may result in milk fever or an abcess, so steps must be taken immediately to alleviate the condition.

The trouble is more likely to occur with small litters when the puppies are obtaining adequate milk supplies without drawing on all the teats. Those most likely to be affected are the back ones which often carry heavy milk yields, and to a lesser extent the front ones may also be affected. The middle breasts do not seem as likely to be involved and are usually those most readily drawn on by the puppies.

As soon as the condition is diagnosed the affected breast should be gently massaged and softened with warm poultices to ease the pressure. Then some of the milk should be drawn off, and when it is flowing freely one of the strongest puppies should be placed on the teat and encouraged to suck. When he has had his fill he should be replaced by another until the breast is clear.

There may be no further trouble once it is soft and pliable, and the puppies may now use it normally. But it must be watched and the treatment repeated if necessary. Once a gland becomes really congested and hard the puppies will avoid it as they are unable to draw the milk from it in this condition, so it is essential to get the milk flowing to avert any possible complications. The dam must also be kept under careful observation to ensure there are no complications as an aftermath of the whelping. Any rise in temperature, refusal of food, vomiting, unhealthy discharge, or diarrhoea should alert the breeder.

There may be retention of a puppy and if this is dead professional help must be summoned without delay; or perhaps the bitch has failed to pass one or more of the afterbirths, in which case an injection to encourage this may be called for, or antibiotics may be necessary. So it is essential to seek advice immediately if any abnormal symptoms such as these should occur.

If there is no infection and no complications, the bitch will usually be happy and relaxed after the birth, and ready to take nourishment, so any signs of discomfort or distress should cause the breeder to suspect something to be wrong, and he should therefore take the necessary steps to obtain advice or help should any untoward symptoms manifest themselves.

Once the puppies are safely born the bitch should be fed generously and this applies to nursing mothers of all breeds as suckling puppies imposes a great strain on the dam.

I give fluid feeds only for the first twenty-four hours. Then for the next twenty-four hours I add semi-solids such as fish, minced meat and eggs. If all is going normally I then gradually revert to ordinary food, simultaneously increasing the quantity given. From about a week after whelping until the puppies are weaned the dam will be fed lavishly with plenty of flesh (raw meat, stewed beef, ox-cheek, offal, sheep's head, paunch, fish, etc.), milk feeds of various kinds, eggs, broth, wholemeal food and vegetables. She also has calcium and cod liver oil, or similar additives.

If the litter is a large one I give three meat feeds and two milk meals during this period. If there are only a few puppies less food will be required, but this must be judged by the bitch's and the puppies' condition and her milk supply. Leave fresh water always available as nursing mothers require ample liquids.

Weaning the Litter

I like to start weaning puppies early to lessen the strain on the dam, and also to make this as gradual a process as possible. Scraped raw beef and enriched milk can be offered at the third week, and at four weeks puppies can be having two small feeds of each of these each day. Other items are then introduced gradually: cooked meat of various kinds, fish, and a variety of milk feeds, plus fine puppy meal or crumbled wholemeal bread. I also add cod-liver oil and calcium or their equivalents daily.

At five weeks mine have five meals a day, three of meat and two milk meals and I continue this until they are eight or ten weeks old. At five weeks I consider puppies to be fully weaned, but the dam is still allowed to visit them if she wishes to, but is never compelled to be with them. In fact from the time of the birth the dam is always free to get out of the box and away from the puppies if she wishes to do so.

Worming and Other Matters

Puppies should be wormed at least twice before sale, and they should not go to their new homes younger than eight weeks old. They should always be accompanied by a diet chart and instructions as to correct care and routine should also be given to the new owner.

Some breeds seem especially subject to worms despite every possible precaution. With my breed I find it necessary to dose at about three weeks old and again ten days later, with perhaps a third worming at about eight weeks old. But other breeds appear to be less susceptible, and it may

be possible to defer the first worming until five or six weeks old, followed by a second dose a week or so later. One point I have observed is that puppies from maiden or young bitches seem to be much more liable to heavy worm infestation, and that as the dams grow older their progeny do not seem to be affected to the same degree.

Indications of worm infestation in young puppies are coat standing on end, hard and distended stomach, unhealthy motions, passing jelly or mucus, and a lack of weight gain. These symptoms may develop at a very early age and it is then advisable to dose without delay. The modern preparations are safe and effective and no fasting is required, and I have found no risk or danger involved in the treatment. Worming does not give puppies permanent immunity but they should remain clear for some weeks, although it may be advisable to repeat the treatment when they are about four months old, and subsequently as and when it appears necessary.

A further point is to keep puppies' nails short and they should be clipped each week to prevent them scratching the dam or catching in the bedding.

If tails must be docked and dew-claws cut these should be done a few days after birth. It is not a difficult job, but it is advisable for the novice to obtain the help of an experienced person to undertake this task. Care should be taken that tails are docked to the correct length as this varies for different breeds.

Some Aspects Concerning Dogs

Only suitable males should be used for breeding, and in addition to the same general requirements of good health and temperament which apply to bitches, the standards required regarding type and quality should, if possible, be even higher. Fewer males are required in a breeding programme, so the elimination process must be even more stringent. With working dogs the same rules of strict selection should also apply.

Those dogs which do not measure up to the desired standard should not be used at stud, and it is a mistaken conviction to assume that every dog should be mated. Apart from other considerations this would not be practical, for numbers would get completely out of control in the dog population, with a rapid increase in 'also-rans' and unwanted puppies.

If a dog is used regularly at stud he generally falls into a pattern of life and does not worry unless a bitch is ready for mating. But a dog which is used only once or twice during his life tends to become awakened but not satisfied, and may well be more frustrated than if not used at all.

Most males settle down after puberty and do not worry unduly, but some breeds or individuals tend to be more highly sexed than others, and if a dog becomes an embarrassment the question of castration should be considered. This course is not generally necessary but in extreme cases it may be the best solution. The worried owner of an oversexed dog may feel that if only he were mated it would calm him, but it will not generally solve any problems and as already suggested the condition will probably be aggravated.

So my advice is that you should accept that your dog will fall into one of three categories: firstly, top dogs to be used for breeding, secondly, other dogs which are kept for various purposes – as companions, as guards or for work. These dogs to remain entire, but not used at stud, and thirdly, dogs which are not suitable for breeding, but

which are difficult and where castration may be advisable.

Care of the Stud Dog

A dog used regularly at stud must be kept in good condition, fit, hard and active. He should not be over-weight, but must be generously fed with a good proportion of protein in his diet. The frequency with which a dog may be used will vary according to a number of factors. Perhaps as a rough guide, the smaller and medium breeds might average two matings a week during the dog's prime when between two and six years old, and this should not tax him unduly. With younger dogs, under two years old, perhaps once a week would be wiser, and the same would apply to those over six years of age. But such suggestions are subject to variation and must be elastic. I have known of dogs used much more frequently without apparent ill effects. With the bigger breeds it would not generally be advisable to use them as frequently as the smaller ones, but the question does not generally arise since they are not usually bred on a large scale in any case.

External considerations of management, handling, condition and the individual dog's potency, etc., must all play their part. If a dog is well cared for and is healthy and virile he may retain his fertility until he is in his 'teens; but this is unusual and not many dogs are still useful at stud after nine or ten years of age.

If a dog mates quickly and easily he can be used much more frequently than another, which requires several attemps to achieve a mating. The latter can lose more energy over one unsuccessful effort than the former would do in mating two or three bitches.

If a dog mates without trouble he will not be exhausted and will be as fit as before; after a little rest he will be ready to enjoy his food and be back to normal. If well managed a dog can be in regular use at stud and still keep in top condition for the show ring.

But conversely, the dog which steams about for prolonged periods, trying ineffectively until he is exhausted, panting and wild-eyed, and with his heart racing, will be far more spent. He is frustrated and upset and probably

will not eat or rest, and these sessions if embarked on
frequently will soon take their toll of a dog's condition.

The Mating

It is best to start a dog at stud when young as this is more
likely to ensure an easy mating, and this could be at about
ten months to a year old for a small dog and perhaps
eighteen months or so for a large one.

It is preferable to commence a maiden dog with a steady
and experienced brood bitch, as a nervy or snappy one can
upset a youngster. A small, empty, enclosed area is usually
best for the mating, where the dogs are not distracted, and
where there are no obstructions to impede matters or to
make the dogs inaccessible if help is necessary.

Usually two people should be present, one to concentrate
on the dog and the other on the bitch. But sometimes with
big powerful dogs or those which are obstreperous, extra
help may be required to steady the animals.

The bitch should be on the lead so she is under control,
but she should be allowed free play to encourage the dog,
and meanwhile the dog should be allowed to make advances
and to gain confidence. The bitch must be the focal point
and the handlers should remain background figures.
Encouragement and praise may be offered, but these
should be given quietly so as not to divert the dog's main
interest from the bitch.

On no account should the dog be scolded or curbed, and
no anger or irritation should ever be apparent during a
mating or potential mating. If the bitch is aggressive she
must be controlled, but this must be done by calming and
soothing her, and by firm handling, or if necessary by
muzzling her, and on no account by roughness or violent
actions.

It is most important that matings are carried out in a
tranquil atmosphere so a dog retains his confidence. If he
is subjected to harshness or to inconsistent treatment, or is
frightened or upset in any way, he may become an unreliable stud dog, easily discouraged, and reluctant to
co-operate with his handler.

It is my considered opinion that many potentially

valuable stud dogs are lost to their breeds, or have restricted opportunities because of mishandling, so it is very important to approach the situation sympathetically.

Sometimes a bitch may suffer from a stricture which makes the mating difficult, or even impossible, so if the dog appears to be striking correctly but does not achieve a 'tie', the bitch should be examined to test if the passage is clear. The small finger, first sterilised and then covered

with a little petroleum jelly as a lubricant, should be
gently inserted into the passage.

If the way is clear the finger will slip in easily, but if an
obstruction is felt it will be necessary to stretch this, or
break it down, to enable the dog to penetrate. This can
generally be done by easing the finger in with a screwing
action, gently pressing and twisting and working it to and
fro. The stricture may consist of a strip of skin across the
passage which will require stretching or breaking down, or
it may be a thickened band ringing the passage which will
need enlarging to allow a way through. If this treatment is
carried out slowly and carefully it does not upset the
bitch, but on no account must it be done roughly.

When the bitch shows signs of being prepared to accept
the dog, by turning her tail, and if the dog tries to mount
her, the handlers should be ready to assist if required. The
one assigned to the bitch should steady her and should be
prepared to hold her firmly with both hands should she jerk
as the dog is mating her. Meanwhile, the other handler
should be watching the dog, ready if necessary to give him
some support if he shows signs of slipping away from the
bitch before he has effected the mating. Once he is mated
he should be kept on the bitch's back for a minute or two
before being allowed to turn, as if not fully 'locked' he may
come away if he turns too quickly.

With some of the smaller dogs it is customary not to
turn them, but they are held on the bitch's back until the
completion of the tie. With some of the larger ones it is
usual to lower the dog beside the bitch as this seems more
comfortable for many big dogs. But most make a complete
turn and remain back to back during the mating, and this
is the normal position. The length of the tie may vary from
five or ten minutes to half an hour or more, but its dura-
tion has no relation to the results.

As they separate after mating I usually raise the bitch's
hindquarters and gently tap the vulva which stimulates the
contraction of the vaginal muscles. As the dogs part there
is sometimes quite a back flow of fluid from the bitch, and I
try and avert this as far as possible. Only a small amount
of semen is required to fertilise the bitch but there is

nothing to lose by taking what precautions one can!

If everything is normal with a satisfactory tie, one mating should be sufficient. But if there are any unsatisfactory aspects, such as the bitch coming into colour again, causing doubts as to the correct timing, if the tie was not a good one, or if perhaps she has a history as an unreliable breeder, then it may be wise to have a second mating.

If a bitch is difficult to get into whelp it is worth trying several spaced matings at three or four day intervals. Try the first one as early as possible, perhaps at seven or eight days; a second one at the normal time of perhaps eleven or twelve days, and another as late as possible, perhaps at fifteen or sixteen days. I have known bitches which do not follow the regular pattern, and which may require mating very early or very late to ensure conception, and this condition may be difficult to recognise and is only discovered and corrected by trial and error. But if a bitch is difficult to get into whelp it is worth trying varying the timing to endeavour to catch her at her most fertile period.

Sometimes there is a difference in height between the animals and it may be necessary to adjust this with a low platform. Usually it is the dog who requires raising, and a board (if necessary on blocks) may be used, preferably covered with a sack or a piece of carpet to give purchase.

Some breeders prefer to mate the smaller dogs on a bench or table and the dog soon becomes accustomed to this. Personally I prefer to mate them on the floor as I find it a natural sequence from the preliminary flirting, but this is an optional decision.

The bitch should be brought to the stud dog when she is ready for mating, and every effort should then be made to effect this. This is particularly necessary if a dog is young and valuable and likely to be in much demand at stud, for it is important to ensure he does not waste his energy and that he is not disappointed, which may undermine his confidence and determination. If a dog is brought in and out to a bitch which may or may not be ready, and if he is tried repeatedly and unsuccessfully, these abortive attempts can be most damaging to his future career at stud. Whereas if he is only introduced to bitches ready for mating and is

given correct assistance, culminating in a successful outcome, he is likely to be fully co-operative and ready to
tackle even the most difficult bitch, and he should become
virtually one hundred per cent reliable.

It is most important that the bitch is never allowed to
bite the dog, and this is even more vital with a youngster.
If a dog is roughly treated by a bitch in his early days, this
may affect him to the extent that he refuses to go near any
other bitch which even growls, so the handler of the bitch
must keep her under control and be sure that this does not
happen.

If a young dog mounts the bitch incorrectly he must not
be checked or restrained in any way but the bitch should
be manoeuvred around towards him, and he should still be
praised and encouraged. To check him would not imply
'Don't do it at that end – do it at this end' – it would
simply mean 'Don't do that'.

I once had the greatest difficulty in handling a young dog
whose owner had been 'training' him by giving him a slap
every time he tried to mount the bitch at the wrong angle,
at the same time scolding him and telling him what a silly
dog he was, and that was not the right way to do it.
Eventually I had to send her right away, out of his sight
and sound as he was thoroughly bewildered by her appar-
ently wanting him to mate the bitch and then giving him a
smack when he tried to do so.

Sometimes a dog is shy and very reluctant to try to
mate a bitch if people are near, but he does eventually
succeed when running with her and while both are free. In
this event it is wise to go quietly towards them once they
are mated and to hold the dog gently, stroking and praising
him quietly, and making relaxed contact, so he becomes
accustomed to human proximity in these circumstances,
and he may thus be willing to accept help on a subsequent
occasion if the necessity arises.

Dogs running together may mate naturally sometimes,
but sooner or later there will be problems and it may not
be possible for the dog to effect the mating without some
assistance. Either there may be a big difference in size
between the animals which will require adjustment, or the

bitch may jerk away at the crucial moment and require steadying. So unless the dog will accept human help, there will come a time when he may fail, so it is important for the breeder to accustom him to being handled.

After the mating the bitch should be shut away quietly for a rest before she is exercised or travels, and I try to avoid her passing water too soon. The dog too, should be put in his bed to relax and unwind for a period, and he should not be returned among other dogs for some time until he has completely settled down, when he can resume his normal life. If he is returned too quickly among other males this may create tension and such mishandling may well precipitate friction.

Final Hints on Management
I have kept stud dogs for many years, and I do not consider that they should be treated any differently from other dogs in their ordinary life, and my experience is that if they are treated normally they will respond normally.

But there are certain aspects which require careful management, and it is important not to inflame possible latent jealousy by allowing situations involving tension to occur.

Well before a bitch reaches the height of her season she must be removed and kept completely away from all stud dogs. If several dogs are running together and are able to see, or sniff, a bitch in season this will understandably cause friction, and possibly aggression and trouble.

I always run my dogs together, and have had as many as six or seven or more mature males mixing freely with each other and an equal number of bitches, all happy and friendly together, and I think when this can be managed dogs are much more contented and well adjusted.

It is sometimes considered that a stud dog must not mix with bitches or he will not mate them, but this has not been my experience, and I have had many very successful stud dogs who have lived as family pack dogs.

But although stud dogs may run together under supervision and in open areas, they should never be confined in small enclosures without somebody in attendance.

Young males of the same age which grow up together may not agree well when mature, as neither may be willing to accept the dominance of the other. But I have found if I grow on one new youngster at a time there is not this problem, as he automatically falls into his position as the junior member of the pack, and is thus integrated into the group. The next new addition to follow on falls into line under him and so on.

But I must add that I would never introduce a new adult male into an established pack and I doubt if this would be acceptable among many stud dogs. Some would mix readily on neutral ground, but they would not willingly accept a strange dog into their home surroundings.

BETTY PENN-BULL

I cannot think of anyone in the world of dogs more capable of writing on the subject of breeding stock than Miss Betty Penn-Bull. Since she can remember Betty has always been immensely interested in dogs. Her literary background enables her to pass on her knowledge in an extremely readable way. Miss Penn-Bull's over-riding desire as a child was to own a dog, but she was never allowed one. Her ambition as a youngster was to make a career with dogs but this too received no support from her family and without any backing she proudly secured her first job aged seventeen. Betty was not able to count on any paid training. It included helping in the house to compensate for lack of experience. After eight kennel jobs gaining experience and having managed to save £35 to start her own kennels, she was fortunate in finding a stable for the equivalent of 25p per week. Single-handed and making every penny count, with trimming, puppy sales, breeding and the use of stud dogs, Miss Penn-Bull built up a strain of Kennelgarth Scottish Terriers who are second to none in the breed here in Britain and anywhere in the world where pedigree dogs are known. Miss Penn-Bull has, since these early days, never been away from dogs and dog shows. She has owned seventeen British champions and bred nine. Betty's home-bred Scottish Terrier Champion Kennelgarth Viking is the greatest top sire ever known, creating a record by siring twenty-three British champions.

J.C.

7 Common Illnesses, Recognition and Treatment BY MICHAEL STOCKMAN

It is not intended that this chapter should do anything other than describe what a healthy dog should look like and what steps should be taken if any definite change in that state of health should appear. It must be stressed that your veterinary surgeon is there to be consulted on any occasion where the trouble is outside the scope of your own capabilities and delay in obtaining professional advice may result in a worsening of symptoms and a more serious illness arising.

Before one can decide whether or not a dog is ill, it is first necessary to know the classic signs of health. In brief terms these are as follows:

a Bright, clear eyes.
b A healthy shining coat.
c A readiness for exercise.
d A good appetite.
e The passage of normal quantities of urine and droppings of normal consistency and colour.

Against this may be listed the signs of abnormality:

a Dullness of either eyes or coat.
b Lethargy.
c Lack of appetite.
d Excessive thirst.
e Excessive scratching.
f Vomiting, diarrhoea and excessive urination.

It is obviously impossible in a single chapter to deal with any but a few of the main problems associated with disease and this I intend to do in alphabetical series.

Accidents
These are usually associated with a painful collision with a car or vehicle, but may be the result of being kicked by a horse. Another accident is the scalded or burnt dog. All these should be examined by your veterinary surgeon as soon as possible and if it is necessary to move a heavy dog it is often possible to carry him on a large blanket. This

will not only make the problem of weight much easier to cope with but will also keep the injured animal warm and help to guard against shock. While on the subject of accidents, it is well to mention that the dog in pain may well react to human attempts to assist by biting. That the helping hand may be the one that normally feeds him is no guarantee of immunity, so approach the injured dog with care. If possible apply a stout leather collar and hold on to it while moving or examining the patient.

Allergies
Many proteins can give rise to allergic reactions which manifest themselves in general by swellings appearing in the skin especially round the face. These symptoms are often referred to under the name of 'nettle-rash' and in most cases disappear as quickly as they arise, usually without treatment. Occasionally it is necessary to give an injection of an anti-histamine drug to counteract the histamine which has caused the allergy.

The cause may be something the dog has eaten, a sting from a bee or wasp or even a vaccine injection. Whatever the reason it is possible that more serious symptoms may arise as a result of the allergic reaction taking place in the lining of the stomach or intestine giving rise to vomiting, diarrhoea or dysentery with passage of blood with loose faeces. Reactions may also take place in the respiratory system producing signs of asthma-type breathing. Both these latter conditions are extremely serious and need very urgent attention from the veterinary surgeon. It cannot be too often stressed that when some urgent condition is apparent it is normally much better to put the patient in the car and drive straight to the nearest surgery rather than waiting for a veterinary surgeon to be contacted on the phone and directed to you. With the advent of multi-man practices running modern hospitals, all the necessary equipment is there to deal with an acute emergency.

Anal Glands
These are two secretory sacs lying just below and to either side of the anal opening. They produce a vile-smelling

protective secretion which in the wild dog presumably
acted as a lubricant to the hard excreta formed by a dog
which ate the skin and bones of its prey as well as the
softer flesh. With softer present-day intake our dogs tend
to pass a softer motion and as a result the glands' function
is partially lost. This causes the sacs to fill up and stretch
the overlying tissue, causing the dog discomfort and
making him attempt to get relief by rubbing his bottom
on the ground or chewing at his hind-quarters with result-
ant patches of wet eczema on the skin of the area. The cure
in simple cases is by digital compression of the glands and
most veterinary surgeons if asked will demonstrate the
technique. If the later stages of eczema or abscessing have
been reached the appropriate professional advice will have
to be sought.

Bladder
The urinary bladder, as its name implies, stores the urine.
Problems in this organ can be those of inflammation or
cystitis with or without bacterial infection, stone-formation
within the urine leading to either irritation or blockage of
the outlet or urethra, or both conditions together. Correction of all these conditions is essentially the task of the
professional man and, especially in the case of a blockage
leading to retention, is urgent in the extreme, requiring a
greater or lesser degree of surgical intervention. Cystitis
itself may need treatment with bladder antiseptics and
antibiotics, as well as adjustment of the diet in order to
lessen the chances of recurrences. Urine samples are
usually needed to assist in making a positive diagnosis and
can easily be obtained from dog and bitch alike if the
collection is left to the time at which the animal is most
ready to relieve itself. Care should be taken that such
samples are collected in dishes and bottles free from all
contaminants such as sugar. The actual technique of
collection is simplified if an old frying pan is used. In the
case of the bitch, give her time to get started before sliding
the pan into place, or she may well stop.

Ears
The treatment of inflamed ears is without doubt one of the
least understood of all first-aid attention required by dogs.
It would, as a generalisation, be better if owners were to
leave sore ears severely alone rather than attempt to put
matters right themselves. The only action that I would
suggest for 'home-doctoring' is the use of a little warm
olive-oil poured into the canal of the ear in order to assist
the dog's attempts to remove wax and other matter which
tends to accumulate as the body's response to inflammation.
Any attempt at mechanical cleaning, however gently per-
formed, is almost certain to lead to painful and worsening
damage to the highly sensitive lining of the external
auditory canal. This in turn makes the dog scratch and rub
the ear all the more and transforms the mild case into the
chronic. There are so many causes of otitis that a proper
examination and diagnosis must be made before effective
treatment can be instituted.

Eclampsia
This condition occurs in the nursing bitch as a result of
lowering of the calcium levels in the bloodstream. The
usual time of appearance is about two to three weeks after
whelping when the bitch is producing the greatest quantity
of milk, but cases are seen from the last week of pregnancy
onwards. The symptoms are characteristic, and include
rapid breathing, muscular tremors, progressing to inco-
ordination and collapse. Total loss of consciousness may be
rapidly followed in untreated cases by death, and help
should be gained with the utmost urgency.

Ecto-parasites
This category includes the four main outside invaders
which attack the dog's skin, namely, fleas, lice, mites and
ticks. All four are unnecessary and every effort should be
made to remove not only the parasites on the body itself
but also those which have temporarily detached themselves
and are in bedding, kennel-walls and the like. The dog-flea
can jump prodigious distances and is not fussy about the
species to be used as a host; so it may well land on human

skin as well as rabbits, hedgehogs and cats. There are numerous effective products on the market, but it is imperative that whatever is used should be employed exactly according to the makers' instructions (which will usually include warnings about keeping substances away from the animal's eyes). Incidentally, unless the label mentions cats specifically, it is better to assume that it is NOT safe as cats are notoriously susceptible to parasiticides. Lice do not move about with anything like the rapidity of the flea, tending to crawl slowly if they move at all, but they are equally capable of getting off the dog and hiding in cracks and crevices. They are particularly fond of attaching in the folds of skin at the rear edge of the ears and may well be missed as a cause of the dog scratching at its ears. In the cases of both fleas and lice as well as mites, the best method of dealing with those which are off the dog's body in kennels is to use a blow lamp on all surfaces before carrying out the usual cleaning with disinfectant agents.

Mites are the basic cause of manges. The common sarcoptic mange (scabies) is capable of great resistance to treatment even with the most modern of drugs. It most frequently attacks the areas of skin with least hair on them and these are obviously under the elbows and in the groin. Spread is usually rapid to other parts of the body, and also to human beings. Treatment under veterinary supervision is essential. Demodectic mange is seen most commonly in the short coated breeds and is associated with congenital infection. The body seems to have some degree of natural resistance to the mite and symptoms in the form of bald areas are first seen at times of stress such as teething in the puppy, heat-periods and whelping in the bitch; in other words the moments when the resistance is at its lowest ebb.

Mites are also found in dogs' ears, the otodectic mange mites, and these are much more common as a source of ear irritation than is generally realised. It is usual to find that the origin of the infection is a cat living in the same household, so it is advisable to treat the family cat if your dog is found to have otodects.

Ticks are normally found in dogs exercised in fields and

do not normally attach in large numbers. They may be removed by bathing in appropriate insecticides, but should not be removed by physically pulling them from the skin; a drop of ether may be used to persuade the offender to let go, but as many ticks are found by the dog's eyes, this may not be possible.

Eyes

It is as well to deal with the subject of eyes under two quite separate headings. The first can be dealt with very briefly as it concerns the eye-balls themselves, in other words the actual organs of sight. If at any time it should be suspected that a dog's sight is in any way disturbed or impaired, the animal should be taken as soon as possible to a veterinary surgeon and in many cases to one who specialises in opthalmology. There is no place whatsoever for any attempt at home treatment except in the event of a hot or corrosive substance being poured accidentally onto the surface of the eye. In most cases it is best to wash the eye immediately with warm water rather than trying to make up a physiologically correct solution of saline. Having removed to the best of one's ability the damaging substance, the dog should then be rushed straight to the nearest veterinary surgeon.

The eyelids themselves which enclose the conjunctival sacs around the eyes may well be rubbed or scratched by the dog as a result of inflammation of the conjunctiva (conjunctivitis) and it is amazing how much damage a dog can inflict on itself in this way, and treatment should aim at preventing further injury until professional help can be obtained. Simple bland ointments or eye-washes, suitable for use in human eyes, will be perfectly satisfactory for this purpose, but it is essential that these should only be considered as first-aid methods and no substitute for proper advice and treatment. Eyes are much too easily ruined for life to take any risks by adopting a policy of wait and see.

Fits

Any form of fit is a serious matter to the owner and, although often very rapid in both onset and recovery, is

none the less frightening to witness, especially when it is the first time a fit has been observed. While the attack is in progress, the animal is best placed in a confined space to reduce the chance of self-damage. It is unlikely that a dog undergoing a fit will bite deliberately, but care should be taken in handling on those occasions where some restraint is necessary to avoid damage to the patient and property. Once the fit has ended, a rest in a darkened room is advisable, and meanwhile veterinary attention should be obtained. Different causes of fits can often be distinguished by use of the readings of an electro-encephalograph and such assistance in diagnosis will enable the veterinary surgeon to recommend an appropriate line of treatment or management of the individual.

Haemorrhage
Any bleeding from a cut surface should be controlled as soon as possible without waiting for professional help. Wherever it is practicable a pressure pad should be applied by means of cotton wool and bandages. If the first bandage does not stop the bleeding put another one over the top rather than remove the first. If the bleeding on limbs is severe, a tourniquet may be applied above the wound by means of a bandage put on tightly. This is merely a first-aid technique and veterinary help should be obtained as soon as possible. Tourniquets should not be left on more than ten minutes without being slackened and reapplied nearer the wound if necessary. Other bleeding points such as those on the body should be treated by holding a pad of cotton-wool firmly in contact with the wound for some minutes. Do not keep removing the pad to see how things are going as this may well dislodge the newly formed clots. If a wound needs stitching it needs stitching as soon as possible, so do not wait till tomorrow, get help now!

Heatstroke
Under conditions of extreme heat which are sometimes met with in the backs of cars held up in traffic jams, a dog may well suffer from heatstroke as evidenced by vomiting, rapid breathing, weakness and collapse. The body temperature

will rise considerably and treatment must begin immediately. Removal to a cool place is obviously the first step and this should be accompanied by the application of cold water to the head and body either by pouring it over the dog or by immersing the animal in a bath. As soon as the animal shows signs of recovery he should be encouraged to drink and meantime should be dried.

Kidneys
The functions of the kidneys are bound up with the elimination of body waste from the blood-stream via the urine. The kidney is a highly complicated filter mechanism. Like all specialised tissues, kidney cells once damaged or destroyed do not repair to their full efficiency. Once their function is lost, they are replaced by fibrous tissue which can take no part in the technical task of the kidney. Many old dogs suffer from varying degrees of nephritis or inflammation of the kidney. While much of this nephritis is caused by a specific infection with Leptospira Canicola, a great deal of extra stress is put on the organs by over-feeding, especially with protein, throughout the dog's life. A great number of dogs in 'good homes' are fed with some degree of over generosity. Giving three pounds of raw meat to four-month-old Alsatian puppies does no good to anyone but the butcher, and puts a tremendous strain on those organs which have to digest and remove the excess protein, in particular the liver and kidneys. This process repeated over a lifetime will inevitably cause harm. As in the case of cystitis, a sample of urine will be required for aiding diagnosis and it may well be that the veterinary surgeon will wish to take a blood sample to estimate the degree of damage present. Advice on treatment will attempt to ensure that the dog's diet is so adjusted to put as little strain on the kidneys as possible and various prepared diets are available on the market to achieve this purpose.

Poisoning
No attempt will be made to discuss this subject in any breadth. Suffice to say that any substance which can possibly act as a poison to a dog should be kept out of his

way. If this policy fails and any poisonous substances are
eaten by a dog, an emetic should be administered as
quickly as possible. Washing-soda or a solution of salt and
mustard in water will usually do the trick, but even if
vomiting is induced, a veterinary surgeon should be consulted as soon as possible for advice as to what further
treatment is needed, if possible taking the packet or its
name for his information. If the animal is already seriously
affected, it is essential that body warmth be maintained
while help is being sought, in order to counteract shock.
In this context, blankets and hot-water bottles are commonly used. While on the subject of poisons, it is as well
to point out that the commonly held opinion that Warfarin
rat poisons are harmless to dogs and cats is entirely wrong.

Skin Diseases
Apart from the ecto-parasitic types mentioned elsewhere,
there are numerous forms of skin troubles. These include
ringworm and bacterial types as well as a host of non-
specific conditions. These are the plague of the average
veterinary surgeon's existence, and their diagnosis requires
considerable expertise. Do not try home cures unless you
are certain that you know precisely what you are dealing
with.

Stomach and Intestines
The whole length of the alimentary canal from mouth to
anus can be involved in varying combinations of inflammatory disorders. The obvious symptoms are vomiting,
diarrhoea, dysentery and constipation. The dog, being a
carnivore and having in the wild a tendency to scavenge
from the carcasses of dead animals, is fortunate in being
provided by nature with great ease in vomiting. If this
were not so, the dog would have a poor chance of survival,
and in many cases a single spasm of vomiting is nothing
out of the ordinary, only a response to a bit of injudicious
feeding. In most cases vomiting dogs will tend to drink
water to excess and it is advisable to remove unlimited
supplies of water from their reach. If boiled water with
glucose added (one tablespoonful to a pint) is made avail-

able in small repeated quantities most dogs will retain it. If after a short period the dog has stopped vomiting it is then reasonable to offer farinaceous foods in the form of ordinary semi-sweet human biscuits or sponge-cakes for a day or two. If, however, the vomiting continues when glucose water is tried veterinary attention should be sought.

Diarrhoea may occur as a symptom on its own or, as is often the case, as a sequel to vomiting. Again some basic irritation of the bowel is usually the cause and starvation along with the availability of small amounts of glucose-water will often be sufficient to allow the inflammatory condition to subside of its own accord. If it should continue for more than a day or if blood should appear in either vomit or excreta, veterinary advice is essential. Some forms of acute gastro-enteritis produce a great deal of blood from both ends of the alimentary canal and are occasionally rapidly fatal. Professional help is therefore needed at once, whatever the hour.

Constipation is not normally a problem in the dog which is intelligently fed and exercised. It is usually associated with the ingestion of bones whether deliberately provided or scavenged. It is surprising how often well-meaning neighbours will throw bones over the fence to a dog. The safest rule to follow when feeding bones to a dog is to give nothing other than raw, beef, leg-bones. Cooking removes the gelatine and renders the bones more brittle. These are the sort that splinter and provide ideal fragments to penetrate the bowel and cause fatal peritonitis. When constipation occurs, as evidenced by excessive unproductive straining and sometime vomiting, liquid paraffin is the drug of choice and should be given at the rate of an ounce to a 40 lb dog. If this does not produce a rapid answer, get proper help.

While on the subject of the stomach, mention must be made of that violent emergency, torsion of the stomach and Bloat. The affected dog will show symptoms of acute distress with attempts at vomiting with no result. This is because the twisting of the stomach shuts off the cardiac

sphincter at the entrance of the stomach and makes it
impossible for the stomach contents to leave the organ in a
forward direction. The abdomen becomes rapidly and
enormously distended and the dog will very soon collapse.
This is possibly the most urgent emergency that can be
seen in the dog other than the road accident case, and no
time should be lost in getting the animal into the nearest
surgery or hospital for immediate remedial steps, preferably getting someone else to telephone ahead and warn
that the emergency is on its way.

Throats
The sore throat syndrome may be the result of pharyngitis
or tonsillitis, or it may be the result of traumatic damage
by sharp bones or needles. One useful way of telling the
difference is that dogs with inflamed throats and tonsils
will show difficulty swallowing and make gulping move-
ments frequently, while the one with needle stuck in its
tongue will in addition paw frantically at its mouth. Either
way, get professional attention and never make any
attempt to remove needles and the like yourself. You are
far more likely to push them on down the throat. Choking
may be caused by a dog swallowing a rubber ball which
lodges behind the molar teeth and occludes the windpipe.
An attempt must be made to remove the object with fingers
and by cutting the ball with scissors to deflate it, but this
is usually very near impossible. Another common cause is
the stick that is thrown for a dog to retrieve. On occasion
the stick will land in the ground rather than on it and the
dog will run head-on into the other end. This will often
result in a nasty wound at the back of the mouth. If this
happens, never ignore the occurrence; have the dog
examined professionally immediately as, apart from anything else, this accident causes considerable shock to the
dog.

Uterus
The bitch's uterus is prone to trouble more frequently than
that of other domestic animals. This is a result of the very
delicate hormonal balance obtaining in the bitch which

causes her to suffer false pregnancies almost as a normal state. Unfortunately the theories that breeding from a bitch will have any effect on her future chances of avoiding either the changes of false pregnancy or the various forms of inflammation of the uterus (metritis, pyometra), are not founded on fact. The suggestion that bitches which have never had a litter are more prone to pyometra than those that have is based purely on the fact that a greater percentage of bitches are in the former category. Owners contemplating mating their bitches should forget the idea that it is for the bitches' good and think first of whether there is a potential market for the possible puppies or not.

Vaccination
Your own veterinary surgeon will inform you of the course of injections which he or she considers most appropriate for your dog or dogs. The diseases which are normally considered are Distemper, Virus Hepatitis and the Leptospira infections. A course of two injections given at the correct ages will give the best possible chance of conferring immunity, and the best advice is that you should consult your veterinary surgeon not later than when the puppy is eight weeks old. You will also get advice as to the correct timing of booster injections and it is unwise to ignore them.

Worms
Until recent years, the worm problem was confined to those types known as round-worms and tape-worms. Now however, there is an increasing incidence of hook-worms and some evidence of whip-worm. It is obviously important to know for certain which particular type is infesting your dog. For this reason it is important to ask your veterinary surgeon to identify a specimen if you are in any doubt as to what it is. Each type of worm needs a different treatment régime and this will include not only dosing the dog with the appropriate remedy, but also dealing with the possibilities of re-infestation. In the case of puppies suffering from the ubiquitous roundworm it is advisable to dose the dam both before breeding from her and once she has weaned the litter.

Finale

If it appears that throughout these notes I have been leading you and your dogs straight into the consulting-room of your veterinary surgeon, I make no apology. When you own a dog or dogs for the first time make it a policy to find a local veterinary surgeon and consult him or her. After the consultation, follow the advice given. If you do you will soon build up mutual confidence and you will receive credit for any knowledge and expertise you will obviously gain. Knowing when you need help, and knowing when you need it urgently are the two pieces of knowledge which will give you the best chance of keeping your dog healthy. If it is at all possible make a habit of taking your dog to the surgery. Many veterinary practices now run efficient appointment systems and in this way you can see the person of your choice and get the greatest benefit of the full equipment of the practice.

MICHAEL STOCKMAN

I invited Mr Stockman to write this chapter for many reasons, but mainly because I know that for many years he has been very interested, spent much time, and worked very hard to get breeders and members of the veterinary profession to work together in every possible way for the good of the dog. Mr Stockman qualified from the Royal Veterinary College in 1949, and spent four years in the Royal Army Veterinary Corps in Germany and Malaya training war dogs as guards, patrols, and trackers. The rest of his professional life has been spent in a mixed general practice. He is married to a veterinary surgeon who, in his own words, does all the intelligent work in the practice. He first showed dogs in 1942 by handling for a number of breeders and exhibitors of Golden Retrievers, Irish Setters, and Bulldogs. He bought his first Keeshond in 1946, but only started showing the breed with any purpose in about 1960. Now, however, when business permits, he can be seen at most leading shows around the Keeshond rings.

J.C.

8 Kennel Club Breed Standard

The general appearance of the West Highland White
Terrier is that of a small, game, hardy-looking Terrier,
possessed of no small amount of self-esteem; with a
varminty appearance; strongly built, deep in chest and back
ribs; level back and powerful quarters on muscular legs,
and exhibiting in a marked degree a great combination of
strength and activity. Movement should be free, straight
and easy all round. In the front the legs should be freely
extended forward by the shoulder. The hind movement
should be free, strong and close. The hocks should be
freely flexed and drawn close in under the body, so that
when moving off the foot, the body is pushed forward with
some force. Stiff, stilted movement behind is very objectionable.

Head and Skull
The skull should be slightly domed and when gripped across
the forehead, should present a smooth contour. There
should only be a very slight tapering from the skull at the
level of the ears to the eyes. The distance from the occiput
to the eyes should be slightly greater than the length of
the foreface. The head should be thickly coated with hair,
and carried at a right-angle or less, to the axis of the neck.
On no account should the head be carried in the extended
position. The foreface should gradually taper from the eye
to the muzzle. There should be a distinct stop formed by
heavy, bony ridges, immediately above and slightly over-
hanging the eye, and a slight indentation between the eyes.
The foreface should not dish or fall away quickly below the
eyes where it should be well made up. The jaws should be
strong and level. The nose must be black. Should be fairly
large, and forming a smooth contour with the rest of the
muzzle. The nose must not project forward giving rise to a
snipy appearance.

Eyes
Should be widely set apart, medium in size, as dark as
possible in colour. Slightly sunk in head, sharp and
intelligent, which, looking from under the heavy eyebrows,

imparts a piercing look. Full or light-coloured eyes are objectionable.

Ears
Small, erect and carried firmly, terminating in a sharp point. The hair on them should be short, smooth (velvety) and should not be cut. The ears should be free from any fringe at the top. Round pointed, broad, large or thick ears are very objectionable, also ears too heavily coated with hair.

Mouth
Should be as broad between the canine teeth as is consistent with the sharp varminty expression required. The teeth should be large for the size of the dog, and should articulate in the following manner:—The lower canines should lock in front of the upper canines. There should be six teeth between the canines of the upper and lower incisors. The upper incisors should slightly overlap the lower incisors, the inner side of the upper incisors being in contact with the outer side of the lower incisors. There should be no appreciable space between the incisors when the mouth is closed ensuring a keen bite; a dead level mouth is not a fault.

Neck
Should be sufficiently long to allow the proper set on of head required, muscular and gradually thickening towards the base allowing the neck to merge into nicely sloping shoulders, thus giving freedom of movement.

Forequarters
The shoulders should be sloped backwards. The shoulder blades should be broad and lie close to the chest wall. The joint formed by the shoulder blade and the upper arm should be placed forward, on account of the obliquity of the shoulder blades, bringing the elbows well in, and allowing the foreleg to move freely, parallel to the axis of the body, like the pendulum of a clock. Forelegs should be short and muscular, straight and thickly covered with short hard hair.

Body
Compact, Back level, loins broad and strong. The chest
should be deep and the ribs well arched in the upper half
presenting a flattish side appearance. The back ribs should
be of a considerable depth and the distance from the last
rib of the quarters as short as is compatible with free
movement of the body.

Hindquarters
Strong, muscular and wide across the top. Legs should be
short, muscular and sinewy. The thighs very muscular and
not too wide apart. The hocks bent and well set in under
the body so as to be fairly close to each other when standing, walking or trotting. Cow-hocks detract from the
general appearance. Straight or weak hocks are undesirable and are a fault.

Feet
The forefeet are larger than the hind ónes, are round,
proportionate in size, strong, thickly padded and covered
with short hard hair. The hind feet are smaller and thickly
padded. The under-surface of the pads of feet and all nails
should be preferably black.

Tail
5 to 6 inches long, covered with hard hair, no feather, as
straight as possible, carried jauntily, not gay nor carried
over the back. A long tail is objectionable and on no
account should tails be docked.

Coat
Colour pure white, must be doublecoated. The outer coat
consists of hard hair, about 2 inches long, free from any
curl. The under coat, which resembles fur, is short, soft
and close. Open coats are objectionable.

Colour
Pure white.

Weight and Size
Size about 11 inches at the withers.

Index